The GOSPEL for PET LOVERS

What the Bible and Animals Teach Us about the
Most Important Message in the World

DAVID J. BRADY

To the Animals…
"Thank you, for all you have taught us!"

"Just ask the animals, and they will teach you.
Ask the birds of the sky, and they will tell you."
Job 12:7, NLT

CONTENTS

Additional Resources:

www.livinginthevertical.com

A WORD TO THE READER

W ho would enjoy reading this book? **Pet-Lovers!** If you fit into that category, I am confident this book will prove helpful to you. I have written this book as a Christian, and I believe that other Christians would benefit from learning more about the Bible's teaching on animals and its relationship to the Gospel; I really wrote this book with another group of pet-lovers in my mind and heart. That group is those who are not Christians—maybe those from another religious tradition or with no religious preference at all. Through the years I have found that pet-lovers from all backgrounds have an incredible and almost instantaneous connection with each other. In fact, I don't think I've ever met a person who loved animals that I didn't like. However, if you are not familiar with the Bible, you might be surprised to learn that God is an animal-lover too. Here are several biblical realities about God and his relationship to animals that you might already agree with:

1. You think animals are a really good idea—so does God. The Bible says, *"God made all sorts of wild animals, livestock,*

and small animals, each able to produce offspring of the same kind. And God saw that it was good" (Genesis 1:25, NLT)._

2. You love animals—so does God. The Bible says, *"For God so loved the world, that he gave his only Son"* (John 3:16a). Certainly, that worldwide love of God is for humans, but it also includes the animals and the entire planet.

3. You think that good pet-owners should care for and protect their animals—so does God. The Bible says, *"The godly care for their animals, but the wicked are always cruel" (Proverbs 12:10, NLT)._

4. Finally, you enjoy your animals so much you cannot imagine any appealing version of the afterlife that does not include them. Jesus is slated to return, bringing His kingdom from heaven to earth, riding a white horse. The Bible says, *"Then I saw heaven opened, and behold, a white horse! The one sitting on it is called Faithful and True..." (Revelation 19:11)._

If you would like to know what the Bible and animals have to teach us about God and His plan for your life, then I encourage you to get a copy of this book and read it. If you are curious to know what the Bible has to say about your pet being in heaven, this book might be an eye-opener for you. Let's get started.

Happy reading!
David J. Brady

INTRODUCTION

Let everything that has breath praise the LORD! Praise the LORD!
(Psalm 150:6)

All creatures of our God and King Lift up your voice and with us sing
Alleluia, Alleluia
(Attributed to St. Francis of Assisi)

Animals are a magnificent gift from God. My wife and I are pet-lovers who have been blessed to share over two decades of marriage with a myriad of animals. With our pets, we have experienced great joy, as well as deep sadness. It's amazing how much we have loved our pets, yet for years their spiritual significance had been unclear to me. I am a Christian pastor who had never reflected on animals through the lens of my faith. I had preached thousands of sermons, and not even one of them had dealt with a scriptural perspective on animals.

Prompted to see what the Bible had to say, I was surprised that I could hardly turn a page without some reference to an animal. In fact, I found approximately one hundred different animals mentioned in the pages of Scripture: everything from fleas to frogs, from geckos to goats, from dogs to donkeys, and from serpents to seagulls. One of the first jobs God gave to our forefather Adam was the naming of the animals in the Garden of Eden, and our lives have been intertwined ever since. As I dug deeper, I realized the Bible not only mentions a wide variety of animals, but it also contains a wealth of wisdom about the importance of our relationship with them.

Despite that wealth of biblical information, many Christians dismiss animals as unimportant. To put it bluntly, they seem to believe animals just don't matter. Because they aren't human, they aren't important. This idea seems to stem from a misinterpretation of the creation story. Humans (men and women) are the pinnacle of God's creation and have been given a special place of honor in that creation. Genesis 1:27 says, *"God created man in his own image, in the image of God he created him; male and female he created them."* However, being created in the *image of God* is not a license to mistreat the rest of creation. Rather, **greater position leads to greater responsibility**. The biblical story of creation does distinguish us from animals, but it also makes it clear that we share a common status as created, earthly beings. When God made the animals, the Bible tells us clearly that He was pleased with what He had made. In fact, animals receive the same joyful stamp of approval from the Maker as the rest of creation. When the Creator inspected His handiwork, He *saw that it was good.*

God's care for all of creation is seen in Jesus' Sermon on the Mount. In Matthew 6:26 he says, *"Look at the birds of the air; they do not sow or reap or store away in barns, and yet your heavenly Father feeds them. Are you not much more valuable than they?"* We often take that verse as a validation of our "more valuable" status, but it also affirms the importance in God's eyes of tiny birds. Animals do matter because they are a wonderful part of God's creation. **Since animals are important to God, they should be important to us.**

Yes, we have been given authority over animals but only under the authority of God. He made them originally, not to be food or work machines but to be reflectors of His glory and greatness. Many of us pet owners have learned that pets are not ever really "owned," but they are entrusted to us. We are called to care for them more as stewards than as owners. The only true and final claim to ownership of everything in creation is the claim of the Creator Himself. He made us and we are His—all of us, even the animals. Psalm 24:1 declares, *"The earth is the LORD's and the fullness thereof, the world and those who dwell therein."*

The Bible contains numerous examples of important life-lessons we can learn by reflecting on the character and actions of animals. For example, King Solomon says, *"Go to the ant, O sluggard; consider her ways, and be wise" (Proverbs 6:6).* This means we can learn how to live more productive lives by observing ants. Ants plan ahead, they store up for the future, they are self-starters, and they are incredibly hard workers. These life-lessons *are* important. However, they are *not* the central message of the Bible.

The central message of the Bible is God's great plan to rescue a perishing people through His Son Jesus Christ. The good news of how He accomplishes this rescue is called the Gospel. In fact, our English word "Gospel" comes from the Greek word *euangelion*, which simply means "good news." The Gospel message can be summarized in three parts: good news, bad news, and good news. The initial **good news** is that God made a pure and beautiful universe, putting humans in charge of the earth as His representatives. The **bad news** is that we rebelled against Him, severing our relationship and bringing sin and death into every corner of the world. The ultimate **good news** is that God did not leave us in our sin and death. He sent his only Son, Jesus Christ, to live a sinless life, to die for our sins on the cross, and to be raised from the dead on the third day.

The Bible distills that bad and good news down to its essence when it says, *"The wages of sin is death, but the free gift of God is eternal life in Christ Jesus our Lord" (Romans 6:23).* The good news of Jesus Christ requires a response. The gift must be received. Each of us must turn away from sinful rebellion, trust Jesus as Savior, and follow Him as Lord. If we have placed our faith in Christ, we can rest assured that our sins have been completely forgiven. We have been adopted into God's family as His children, and He has promised that we will live with Him forever. That's the Gospel!

This Good News has been the central message of Christianity since the resurrection of Jesus on Easter Sunday almost 2,000 years ago. Many messages are here today and gone tomorrow but not the Gospel. It has a timeless relevance for all generations because it is the *only* message that is "the power of God for salvation." My grandfather J. Clyde Yates was born in the late 1800's and spent sixty years as a pastor. What message did he preach? The Gospel! He believed this Gospel to be of such vital significance that he wrote, "We must dedicate every drop of our blood, every fibre of our being, and every vestige of our influence to the tremendous task of making the message of Jesus known to all men." I agree with my grandfather. I have found the truth of the Gospel to be deeply compelling and the beauty of the Gospel to be deeply satisfying. That's why I have written **The Gospel for Pet-Lovers**. For me, bringing together these two passions, pets and the Gospel, has been a great joy. It will be an even greater joy for me, if through this book, you come to know and love *both* God and your animals in a more profound way.

The book follows the outline of an animal's life as the structure for its chapters. It begins with the birth of an animal and moves through the stages of its life to its death. However, that is not the end. In the final chapter entitled "What's Next?" I look at a question that many pet owners have pondered, "Will my pet be in heaven?" If you are familiar with the Bible, you will recognize that I reference passages from all of its parts. This is because I believe the Bible to be a book that is breathed-out by God through human authors. In other words, it *is* the word of God. It is completely true and trustworthy. It has authority over all human authorities. Therefore, I am convinced that greater familiarity with the Bible is essential and beneficial for everyone. That's why I suggest you read this book with an open Bible or Bible software program. There are many Bible passages I discuss in the book, but I do not explain their full context. You will benefit greatly by reading the verses in context. Your understanding will be stronger and more vivid. Any good modern translation will do, but I primarily quote from the English Standard Version (ESV) and secondarily from the New Living Translation (NLT). If no translation is indicated, assume it to be the ESV.

I also hope you will consider using this book as a discussion guide for a small-group gathering. My suggested format would be to discuss first the "pet topics" and then the related passages from the Bible. Going through such a process in a group setting will deepen the learning and enjoyment of the biblical themes presented in this book. Additionally, there are resources at www.livinginthevertical.com, which can facilitate your private study or the study of a small group.

I am on a journey. This book recounts a few steps of that pilgrimage. Somewhere along the way, I learned that both God's world and God's Word are great teachers. They are designed to introduce us to God himself. Knowing Him is life. He is the purpose of the journey. I met Him in Jesus Christ. I have peace with Him through the cross. The Gospel of Christ Jesus is the greatest news my ears have ever heard. I desire to share it with you. I am still on a journey. My simple invitation, "Will you join me? "

A Prayer of Blessing

Dear Heavenly Father,

Thank You for the very good gift of our animals.

They bring us much joy and companionship.

Give us the wisdom and resources we need to care for them well.

Help us to read this book with open hearts and to learn the lessons

You are teaching us through our pets and through Your Word.

In Jesus name,

AMEN

Chapter One

BORN
Looking at Our Pets with New Eyes

By what means is God made known unto us? We know him by two means:

First, by the creation...which is before our eyes as a most elegant book,

in which all creatures, great and small, are as so many characters

leading us to contemplate the invisible things of God...

Second, he makes himself known to us more openly by his holy and divine

Word, as much as we need in this life, for his glory and

for the salvation of his own.

(Belgic Confession, Article Two)

Animals point us to God. They lead us to contemplate Him. Really? Yes. Because God made them, we can see Him through them. We observe God's awesome power, enjoyment of diversity, love of beauty, sense of humor, and desire for relationships as we look at them. All aspects and stages of our pets' lives are windows into the mind and heart of their Creator. It is God who made the horse that can run like the wind, the dog that can track the faintest smell, and the cat that can climb the highest tree (I'm not so sure what happened with the getting down part). We have a deep appreciation for the character and abilities of our pets such as loyalty, playfulness, or athleticism—all of which point to the goodness and greatness of the One who made them.

Animals are great teachers, beginning with the miracle of their birth and continuing all the way to the mystery of their death. The Bible says in Job 12:7, *"Ask the beasts, and they will teach you; the birds of the heavens, and they will tell you."* Birth is one of those "holy" events in life where the veil between the eternal and the temporal is thinnest and where we see the hand of God most clearly. It is where we wait while God works. It humbles us by showing us that even though we are not in control of the world around us, God is.

In the early 1990's my wife and I were graduate students in Texas and headed toward conventional lives. God led us to buy a farm in a rural community and to find jobs near the homestead. We were fascinated with the idea of growing our own food, of enjoying fresh country air and water, and of being able to have horses and other animals. We mulled the idea over and over in our minds until God opened a door for us to buy a former tobacco farm in North Carolina. That began a great adventure on our farm, named Shadowlands, which has provided us with a place to have many precious animals through the years. In short order, we were blessed with a couple of horses, one of which was a middle-aged thoroughbred mare named Kahlua in need of a good home. My wife had owned and ridden horses during her childhood, but she never had the opportunity to have a foal of her own. Now we were excited at the prospect of having a foal on Shadowlands.

We bred Kahlua, who easily became pregnant, and we settled in for the long eleven month gestation. As Kahlua's time drew near to deliver her foal, Jennifer and I took care to make every necessary preparation for the little one's arrival. As her due date drew nearer, we brought her into the barn attached to our house each night. Being first-time horse parents we were very concerned and wanted everything to go smoothly. We installed a baby monitor in the barn with the video-feed going into our bedroom. We hardly slept. It was awful. We were awakened every time the horse snorted, sneezed, ate, drank, pooped, or even moved. We were determined to be there if there were any complications.

Our excitement began to turn to anxiety as day after day passed with no foal. We realized that if something went wrong, our vet lived too far away to be present during an emergency. We read our brood-mare book, and it only gave us more "to fret about." Eventually, Kahlua was two weeks over-due, and we were exhausted from lack of sleep and irritable from the never-ending wait. Each day seemed like a year. Imagine how *she* must have felt.

As Monday March 27, 2000 dawned, we had no idea what that day would hold for us. Kahlua looked as if she was about to explode, but she gave no signs the baby was coming. I had been staying at home as much as possible, but that evening I felt comfortable enough to venture out to a meeting at church, leaving Jennifer home alone in charge of foal patrol.

Several hours later I came home to find Jennifer with the most weary and strained expression on her face that I had ever seen in all the years I'd known her. She looked at me blankly and mumbled, "The filly was born while you were gone."

I said, "That's wonderful, but what's the problem?"

Jennifer replied, "It was a nightmare; Kahlua was cast during the delivery." If you are not a horse person, "being cast" means that while lying down in a stall, a horse turns upside down and gets stuck against the wall. That's right—a thousand pound animal stuck upside down. This is a frightening situation that can become quite dangerous

17

for the horse and for the human who tries to help—add to that picture the unthinkable—delivering a baby horse while the mother is
cast. That was the nightmare scenario Jennifer had just experienced.
It had all happened so fast and furiously, and just as we feared, the
vet was unable to get there in time. Jennifer, along with her friend
Cynthia, had to handle the situation entirely on their own: Kahlua
being cast, the filly coming out, Kahlua struggling mightily to stand
up, and fearing that the baby horse would be trampled.

Under the direction of the vet on the phone, Jennifer delivered
the filly in the stall, tied off the umbilical cord with her shoelace, and
cut it with a kitchen knife. The filly was pulled into the barn aisle and
handed to Cynthia, who had just arrived. Jennifer hurriedly re-en-
tered the stall to help the mother to get righted by tying a rope around
the leg closest to the wall. She made a couple of attempts to pull
Kahlua's legs over, but Jennifer kept slipping on the amniotic fluid.
At that moment Kahlua, in a final act of desperation, exerted a thun-
derous kick, knocking out the boards between the stalls and leaping
to her feet. She landed on the spot where the new baby had been only
moments before. That's when I came strolling leisurely into the picture. I know some of you women are saying, "Typical man!"

The struggle was not over yet. The foal was hungry and was des-
perately trying to find a teat to latch onto. Her traumatized mother
wanted no part of that. When the foal came near to nurse, Kahlua
would run to the other side of the stall. This game of hide and seek
went on and on, and we were growing more and more frustrated.
Finally, when the baby got close enough to grab on to a teat, Kahlua
squealed and kicked her baby, sending the foal flying across the stall
and smack into the wall. We rushed over to the baby horse and found,
unbelievably, that she was unharmed. This poor filly had been alive

for less than an hour and had already experienced two near-brushes with death. We thanked God and asked Him to calm Kahlua and to allow her baby to feed. Miraculously, God answered our prayer. Before too long, we were watching a happily nursing filly. Jennifer and I, on the other hand, were about to collapse from exhaustion.

This event taught us we are never really in control of anything in this world. We planned and prepared for every eventuality, but when birth came upon us, it showed us that we were powerless in the face of such an awesome mystery. We saw through the veil and realized that any sense of ultimate control over the world around us was an illusion, yet we also realized there was an unseen hand—guiding and providing for us through it all. We had been made to wait and wait...

Waiting taught us to slow down and to think carefully about what was happening. We had been forced to handle a dangerous birth, showing us we are always in God's hands even when we can't see them. God used this birth to "break" us. He broke us of a controlling spirit and of an attitude of self-sufficiency. Up to that point we felt stronger and more in control of our lives than we really were. We are profoundly grateful for the lessons God taught us through this birth. We did not want to forget the spiritual truths we had learned, so we named our precious little filly, Isabel, which means "consecrated to God."

My first sight of Isabel filled me with amazement. Her body was so small and her legs were so long. Her front legs practically touched each other because she had no chest, but she was beautiful and perfectly made. She was full of energy and life. Even more curiously, she loved humans from the start. Maybe it was because Jennifer was the first thing she saw, but ever since her birth, she has had a great affection for people. Isabel has always been ready to exchange kisses with any willing partner. We've had the joy of watching her learn to nurse, walk, and run. We've seen her grow up and grow strong and learn how to be ridden. Even on the surface, it has all been fascinating to watch, but was *more* going on than one might suppose?

If God designed our horse Isabel, maybe I could see something in her that would point me toward Him? The Bible says in Psalm 104:24, *"O LORD, how manifold are your works! In wisdom have you made them all; **the earth is full of your creatures."*** Isabel is one of God's creatures—that in wisdom—He has made. She is one of God's many marvelous works. Her birth was one of those precious opportunities beckoning me to ponder and praise her Creator. The Bible says in Romans 1:20 that God's, *"Invisible attributes, namely, his eternal power and divine nature, have been clearly perceived, ever since the creation of the world, in the things that have been made."* My horse, your dog, our cat, and everything else in creation are windows through which we can perceive the power and nature of God. As the hymnist Isaac Watts wrote in <u>I Sing the Mighty Power of God</u>, *"There's not a plant or flower below but makes Thy glories known."* Somewhere deep within all of us, we know that the creation is not the accidental product of chance but the wise and wonderful work of a creator. You may have the privilege of observing roly-poly piles of puppies, nosy kittens, and pushy ponies. They are all declaring the glory, the joy, the wisdom, the goodness, and the power of God.

If our animals are such great windows into the goodness and greatness of God, why do we so often fail to see Him through them? The same passage just quoted from Romans 1 says in verse 18 that all of us in, *"unrighteousness suppress the truth."* The problem with the existence of an all-powerful designer, creator, and sustainer is that He can call the shots. He determines right from wrong and demands obedience; we hate having anyone over us. Our preferred form of rebellion is suppression of the truth about Him and everything He has made. In other words, we ignore God. One of the consequences of this "unrighteous" suppression is spiritual blindness to the amazing realities all around us. We all have a built-in knowledge of God, but the Scripture makes it plain that we have ignored Him and rebelled against Him. Romans 1:21 diagnoses the spiritual condition of all humanity when it says, *"For although they knew God, they did not honor him as God or give thanks to him, but they became futile in their thinking, and their foolish hearts were darkened."*

When we are ungrateful and disobedient, we fall into spiritual darkness, so that in seeing, we do not see. We just do not get it. Looking at our pets, we can only see the surface reality of their existence; in truth, they are the remarkable handiwork of a loving Creator. They are God's calling cards, declaring His existence, character, and power. They point to something outside of and beyond themselves.

The Bible teaches us that all creation, not just animals, is continually shouting out the praise of its Creator. A good example is Psalm 19:1, which reads, *"The heavens declare the glory of God, and the sky above proclaims his handiwork."* This is important to understand. As we said before, the created world and everything in it are windows into the heart and mind of the Creator. That is why we are awed at the sight of a vivid rainbow, a full moon, or a gorgeous sunset. That is also why we melt in tender amazement at the perfection of a little baby, fearfully and wonderfully knit together by God in the mother's womb.

Let us consider a creation of God that is a bit closer at hand. In fact, just look at *your* hand. It is an incredible creation. It can lightly caress or powerfully punch. It can play a piano or scale a mountain. It can nimbly pick up a piece of paper or stoutly hoist a boulder. In other words, you do not have to look very far to see a natural wonder;

you are a natural wonder. The eyes with which you read these words and the ears with which you hear them are creation miracles almost beyond description. In this, God is making Himself known to us, "By the creation, preservation and government of the universe; which is before our eyes as a most elegant book" (Belgic Confession, Article two). However, we often live completely blinded by our sin to the true meaning of that "most elegant book" of creation.

Even if we recognize the wonder of our animals, we face the temptation of granting them the wrong place in our lives. They point us to God; they are not gods. That reminds me of the humorous adage with which all cat owners can immediately concur, "Thousands of years ago people worshipped cats as gods and today our cats won't let us forget it." Seriously, we who love our pets always need to remind ourselves that we were made to worship the Creator and not the creation. God alone deserves first place in our hearts.

If creation is often misinterpreted because of our sinfulness, what can we do about it? If we are in spiritual darkness, how can we move into spiritual light? Psalm 36:9 says of God, *"For with you is the fountain of life; in your light do we see light."* Where do we find this fountain of life-giving light? The answer is the Bible, God's holy and divine Word. Psalm 119:105 makes this clear when it declares, *"Your word is a lamp to my feet and a light to my path."* If we are in the dark about the meaning of creation, we need to turn humbly to the Bible to see clearly.

The beautiful statement from the Belgic Confession that calls the universe "a most elegant book" goes on to speak about the purpose of God's second book, the Bible, by which He, "Makes himself known to us more openly by his holy and divine Word, as much as we need in this life, for his glory and for the salvation of his own." In other words, the Bible helps us to see *more* than if we simply observed the world around us. Like a pair of corrective lenses, it helps us to see the world more clearly and accurately. We can see our animals for what they truly are, wonderful creations, *"Declaring the glory of God and proclaiming His handiwork"* (Psalm 19:1). The darkness is dissipated. We begin to see God more clearly and truly, we see our pets more clearly and truly, we see ourselves more clearly and truly, and we give all the honor and praise to Him and to Him alone.

Like the animals, we humans are "born" by the creative power and will of God. However, people, not animals, need a spiritual re-birth to be taken out of darkness and to be brought into the light. God uses His Word to bring about this re-birth as He states in 1 Peter 1:25, *"You have been born again, not of perishable seed but of imperishable, through the living and abiding word of God."* His Spirit animates His word. The Spirit changes our hearts so that God's Word falls on freshly tilled and fertile soil. Titus 3:4-5 speaks of the Holy Spirit's role in our re-birth saying, *"When God our Savior revealed his kindness and love, he saved us, not because of the righteous things we had done, but because of his mercy. He washed away our sins, giving us a new birth and new life through the Holy Spirit..."* (NLT). Because of these powerful truths, let's trust God's Spirit to teach us as we put on the lens of Scripture. Let's begin to look at our animals through new eyes, as "characters leading us to contemplate the invisible things of God" (Belgic Confession, Article 2).

Isabel with her mother Kahlua

Adolescent Isabel

Isabel, all grown up, with her mother Kahlua

Isabel Running

Jennifer and Isabel

Jennifer, Isabel, Fiona, and Burrito

Chapter Two

LOST
The Heart of the Shepherd for the Lost

What man of you, having a hundred sheep, if he has lost one of them, does
not leave the ninety-nine in the open country, and go after
the one that is lost, until he finds it?
(Luke 15:4)

Have you ever lost an animal? I have. Unfortunately, this has happened on numerous occasions and every time it does, I feel guilty and afraid. Two of our dogs are hound mixes, named Rupert and Fiona. They are trackers! If they catch the tiniest whiff of any interesting intruders into our yard, they pursue them with relentless and reckless abandon. We learned early on we could not train that instinct out of them, so we researched fencing options and decided on an invisible fence. The dogs are supposed to wear a special electric collar that shocks them if they come too near the perimeter of the yard. The shock is unpleasant but not harmful. They can be trained to respect this fence, and it gives them a strong incentive not to cross the line. It takes a bit of effort to teach them where the boundaries are and the consequences for violating those limits. Unfortunately, there have been times when I have been too lazy to put their collars on, and they have run away. However, on a few occasions they have ignored the shock as they blazed through the fence, fast on the heels of a deer or some other irresistible temptation.

One such incident took place on a cold winter's night. The snow had covered the warning flags that outline the yard's edge, and as soon as I let them go out to the bathroom, I regretted it. They saw some creature and shot after it like a bullet, never breaking stride as they crossed the fence and were gone into the dark, snow-covered farmland. They knew better. They were wearing their collars and must have felt the shock as they ran through the fence, but they did not care. Usually, they returned within minutes or at most after an hour or two but not that night. I called and called to no avail. They were gone. All that we provide for them was not incentive enough to keep them home. They were prone to wander, and that's what they were doing.

Jennifer was out of town that night, and all the responsibility was on me. I went inside every so often to warm up, but I would then go back outside to call them some more. My concerns were heightened because of the snow. I realized the damage that could be done to their paws, and maybe their lives, because of the extreme cold and the difficulty they might have in finding their way home. The snow had covered most of the sights and smells that could lead them back home. I continued calling for hours until my voice finally gave out. I grew more anxious with each passing minute. It was now about 2 AM, and they had been gone for five hours.

I thought I heard a faint cry coming from the darkened distance, and I decided I could no longer wait for them to come home. I was going to go after them. They were lost, and I determined to try and find them. They were mine, and I was responsible for them. If they wouldn't or couldn't come home, I was going to go after them. I started off in the general direction of the cry. In a sparsely inhabited region such as ours, one of the most striking features is how dark the night can be. Moonlight is your only hope of seeing, and there was not much of it that evening. I trudged through briar-filled woods, across creeks, and over open fields but found nothing. When I was about to despair, I heard that whimper-like cry. Immediately, I was re-energized to continue my search. I sensed that something was nearby, and in an instant my two dogs were running up to me with tails wagging, as if to say, "Hey, fancy meeting you here." I wanted to yell at them, but I was too overwhelmed with the joy of finding them. All I could do was drop to my knees and embrace them. It was only then I realized I had forgotten to bring their leashes. I had found them, but how was I going to get them home without their running away again? Inevitably, we would come across a rabbit or a deer, and they would be off to the races. The male dog Rupert is very athletic, but since he is a follower and not a leader, I decided to carry Fiona. Hopefully, Rupert would stick with us. The plan worked with only one serious problem; Fiona weighs about forty pounds. I soon realized that carrying forty pounds in the snow, across creeks, and through thick woods is exhausting. I was gasping for breath, and my arms felt like they were going to break, but I had determined not to quit until my runaways were safe at home. We plodded through the dark until we finally saw the light of our house. A few minutes later I took them through the front door. Carefully looking them over, I saw that they were both scratched from running through the underbrush and were completely worn out, but otherwise, they were safe. They were home and I was happy.

As I reflect on that night, I realize that it parallels a Gospel story told by Jesus. He begins his parable with a question that touches the hearts of all animal-lovers. Jesus asks, *"What man of you, having a hundred sheep, if he has lost one of them, does not leave the ninety-nine in the open country, and go after the one that is lost, until he finds it?" (Luke 15:4).* Imagine that your pet is lost. You wouldn't be able to rest until you had found it. Jesus continues the story, *"And when he has found it, he lays it on his shoulders, rejoicing. And when he comes home, he calls together his friends and his neighbors, saying to them, 'Rejoice with me, for I have found my sheep that was lost'" (Luke 15:6).* Did you notice how happy the shepherd is when he finds the sheep and brings it safely home? The shepherd is motivated, not only by *duty* to look after the sheep, but also by *delight* in the sheep.

We were created by God to live in loving relationship with Him. God as our Creator set one boundary, namely, not eating from the tree of the knowledge of good and evil. Like my dogs, we shot over that boundary into the cold, dark night of sin, and we were lost. Into that darkness God sent His Son, the Good Shepherd, to seek us out and to bring us home. When He does, He rejoices! This is the central message of Christianity, the Gospel, the "good news" of the lost being found.

Long before Jesus rescues us, Genesis the first book of the Bible, records our creation. This story begins with God declaring, *"Let us make man in our image, after our likeness. And **let them have dominion** over the fish of the sea and over the birds of the heavens and over the livestock and over all the earth and over every creeping* *thing that creeps on the earth" (Genesis 1:26)*. Men and women are the only creatures made in God's image. To be made in the image of God is a profound reality. God imprints men and women with his nature and sets them apart with incredible potential and responsibility. Among other things, to be made in the image of God means that we are created as uniquely rational, moral, and relational creatures. We are made to excel in everything good and godly. Even if we discussed being made in "the image of God" for hundreds of pages, we would barely begin to scratch the surface of what it means. After we are told that we are made in God's image, the very next words declare, *"And let them have dominion over"* all the animals. Interestingly, the very first attribute of being in God's image is not how we look, but what we are called to do and how we are to do it. What is that? **We are called to have dominion over the animals and the entire earth.**

I know animal-lovers that cringe when they hear this verse because it is often used as a justification for the cruel abuse and inhumane slaughter of animals. They only know the word "dominion" as a synonym for "domination." It is true that dominion can manifest itself in the form of greedy, selfish, and careless treatment of animals or others, but that is not inherent in the meaning of the word dominion. When dominion is characterized by harsh ruling, it is a reflection of the character of the one misusing dominion. God's purpose for dominion is that we rule over the animals, reflecting to them love, wisdom, compassion, and godly justice. The Bible teaches us that mankind has been given dominion over the works of God's hands. God put all things on earth under the authority of humanity. We, men and women, are little kings, called to rule as good representatives of the Great King, who is God. In other words, to be made in

God's image means not only do we have vast powers and rights in this world, but also we have great responsibility for this world. We are given the weighty task of caring for the animals and the planet in a way that honors God our Creator. When I think about this idea of dominion, it helps me to realize I am responsible for my pets, but they are not responsible for me. Much of the suffering of animals comes because of our actions. They are linked to us, and they either suffer or they are blessed by the kind of "rulers" we are. The condition of the one ruled often reflects the character and decisions of the one ruling. For example, when a president or prime minister is a bad person or makes bad decisions, it affects everyone in that nation. Being a ruler is a responsibility filled with both promise and pitfalls.

Immediately, the question comes to mind, if we are made in the image of such a good and powerful King, why is our world in such a mess? The Bible holds the answer. Even though we were created to be virtuous, our sin has made us vile. Ecclesiastes 7:29 declares, *"God created people to be virtuous, but they have each turned to follow their own downward path" (NLT)*. God, as creator and owner of everything and everybody on this planet, has the right to tell us what we can and cannot do. We read in Genesis 2:16-17 that the, " *LORD God commanded the man, saying, 'You may surely eat of every tree of the garden, but of the tree of the knowledge of good and evil you shall not eat, for in the day that you eat of it you shall surely die.'"* Did you notice that God commands man both positively *and* negatively? God gives Adam a free reign to enjoy the full range of natural food delights in the garden. At the same time, God draws a limiting fence around the tree of the knowledge of good and evil. God gives permission on the one hand and pronounces a prohibition on the other. It is that line of prohibition the Serpent will soon tempt Eve to cross, and she will, with Adam docilely following her lead.

Some people can't believe that God would be upset by such a small infraction as eating prohibited fruit. The point is not the specific temptation to which they fell, but the heart of rebellion it manifests. We all can relate to the kind of heart that has a million blessings yet will not be satisfied without the one thing it can't have. Adam and Eve showed their lack of trust in the goodness of their King. They agreed with the tempter that God was withholding some good thing from them, so they rebelled against the clear and simple command of God. They thought they knew better than God. It is that same human arrogance which has brought massive pain and destruction into the world. Rather than trusting and obeying God, we joined Satan in his failed coup d'état.

We willingly turned away from obedience to the High King and sought to set ourselves up as kings, not under Him, but in the place of Him. **Rebellion against God is called sin, and sin brought death into the world.** Death is not a natural part of the world's order. Death is the result of our stupid, selfish, shortsighted, and sinful rebellion. The Bible teaches us this sad reality when it says, *"Sin came into the world through one man, and death through sin, and so death spread to all men because all sinned" (Romans 5:12).* I know this is hard to hear, but it is vitally important in order to make sense of why so much *in* us and *around* us is a broken mess. We see the implications this has for animals and the earth. We humans still have dominion because of our God-given powers, but we often use those powers in selfish and cold-hearted ways that do not represent the goodness of God. **The entire planet suffers as a result of our sin.**

Our sin led to banishment from that earthly paradise called Eden. God cannot and does not allow rebellion in His presence, so we were rightly cast from Paradise into a world of toil. God set angels with flaming swords as guards to prohibit our *unholy* return into His *holy* presence. The gap between God and us was bilateral. The gap was caused, not only by our sin, but also by His purity. Allowing us back into His glorious presence in our filthy condition would result in our immediate incineration. The unbridgeable chasm was set. **No effort on our part could ever bring us back into right relationship with Him.** We were lost in the world without God and without hope.

One of the most dangerous conditions is to be lost, all the while thinking we know exactly where we are. In order for us to hear and receive the good news of salvation in Jesus Christ, we must first understand and acknowledge the bad news of our "lostness" in sin. In terms of God's stated boundaries, how are you doing? Are you safely inside the lines of obedience or have you trespassed and left the yard by breaking God's *positive* and *negative* commands? For example, God clearly states in His Ten Commandments that we are to have no other gods before Him. He will accept no rivals for His unique position as our Creator and King. We must reject all rival claimants for His Throne, whatever or whoever they may be: self, family, ambition, profession, money, pets, or any other pseudo-god. We must not allow anything, even a good thing, to claim first place in our lives. **God and God alone must be first.** As the Supreme Ruler, He is the only one who can determine right from wrong. If we step where He has told us not to, we must be ready to face the consequences for our deliberate rebellion. God *prohibits* hate, murder, lust, adultery, stealing, lying, and coveting. His *positive* commands include love, faithfulness, hard work, truth telling, and contentment with what we have.

Have you ever failed at any of these points? Most of these points? All of these points?

The Bible says if we fail to keep God's law in one area, we have failed the entire test. I, like my dogs, deliberately ran into the cold dark night and could not find my way back home. I was lost. What about you? Where are you this night? The Bible clearly states, *"All we like sheep have gone astray; we have turned—every one—to his own way" (Isaiah 53:6).* You will not be found until you acknowledge that you are lost. If you do not recognize your sinful condition, and if you rebelliously continue to hang on to the lie of your own goodness, you cannot receive God's gift of rescue.

At this point, my mind turns back to that cold night when my dogs ran away. The turning point in the story was not *their choosing* to come home but *my choosing* to search for them. That's when the story turns from the bad news of their being lost to the good news of a person determined to find them. Our human rebellion is universal, *"For all have sinned and fallen short of the glory of God" (Romans 3:23b).* However, that is not the final word. We *do not*, and indeed *cannot*, find our way home, but God sent forth His Son to be born of woman. He came on a rescue mission, *"To seek and to save the lost."* **Wherever you are at this very moment, call out to Jesus, the Good Shepherd. He *will* find you!**

Chapter Three

RESCUED
Saving Our Animals

And of every living thing of all flesh, you shall bring two of every sort into
the ark to keep them alive with you. They shall be male and female.
Genesis 6:19

We have all felt that overwhelming need to rescue an animal in trouble. They are all around us. We come across such animals in traffic, in abusive or neglectful homes, or sitting in an animal shelter. All kinds of animals find themselves in danger: dogs, cats, deer, turtles, and birds. In fact, the list is as long as the kinds of animals that exist. There they are, in trouble, and they need help. Animal-lovers often have touching and dramatic stories of reaching out to rescue those in danger.

I have been involved in many animal rescues through the years, not because I am particularly compassionate, but because I am married to a woman with a huge heart and a determination to help any and all in need. This has been both a wildly fantastic and a wildly frustrating experience. How many times have there been turtles in the road on the way to church and my wife Jennifer must stop and rescue each and every one. Sometimes I get to the point of saying, "Honey, let's leave that one; we're already late for service" (remember, I'm the pastor). That's when I brace myself for an impassioned sermonic rebuke. I already have the points of the sermon memorized. *One*, that animal is in need. *Two*, we can help. *Three,* are you sure you want to be more concerned about getting to church on time so that you can *tell* people about being loving and compassionate Christians, or do you actually want to *be* one? Ouch! That gets me every time.

These animal rescues have been a part of our relationship from the very beginning. In the first year of our marriage, we had planned a two-day winter getaway to the mountains. On the way up to the small town where we intended to stay, on the side of the highway I saw a bridge that went halfway across a river and ended. I was fascinated and turned the car onto the side road to go toward it. Jennifer warned me that she saw a couple of dogs near the bridge. When we got out, we found a pair of starving hunting dogs. The two were very sweet, but they were "nothing but skin and bones." The male dog was bigger, more energetic, and very protective of the female dog. We didn't know how they got there. They were miles away from the nearest house. Our attention quickly moved from the bridge to the dogs and trying to find a way to help them. We were headed to find a hotel in a resort town. We couldn't take them with us. We headed back to the nearest community and bought them some food. It was a very cold day, so we also bought a bale of straw for bedding. We asked if anyone were missing dogs, but no one was. When we got back to "the bridge to nowhere," the dogs ravenously ate their food. We made a bed of straw to help them stay a bit warmer in the extremely cold temperatures. Reluctantly, we said goodbye, dissatisfied with the help we had given, but stymied as to what more we could do.

With heavy hearts we pressed on to our intended destination, the Georgia mountain town of Helen. When we arrived in the town of Helen, it was late afternoon, and we set about finding lodging for the night. To our surprise it was the weekend for some Bavarian festival, and every hotel we checked was fully booked. We looked for hours to no avail. Eventually, we came to the obvious conclusion that there just was "no room in the inn." It was dark and cold, and a drive of several hours back to our home in South Carolina lay before us. We had no other option. This trip was looking more and more like that bridge we had seen earlier in the day. It was becoming in our mind a wasted trip, a trip to nowhere, with no purpose, except maybe to teach us to make hotel reservations in advance.

As we wound our way down the mountain, an undeniable conviction slowly dawned on us. We had to stop and check on those dogs. By that time of night, the temperatures had fallen well below freezing. When we arrived at the dogs' riverfront bed of straw, we saw the male dog standing there like a sentry at his post. The car lights beamed on him, but he didn't move. We kept the car running and the lights shining so we could check on them. When we got to the straw bed, we looked over the edge. There in the middle was the female dog being suckled by the cutest pile of puppy flesh you have ever seen. Since we had left them earlier in the day, this momma had given birth to seven, yes, seven hound-dog puppies on one of the coldest nights of the year. With almost no discussion, we knew what had to happen: momma and puppies were placed in the floor board of the passenger side, daddy dog was piled on Jennifer's lap in our small Honda, and all eleven of us came down the mountain that cold night. Arriving home a couple of hours later, our little Honda "felt and smelt" more like an ark than an automobile.

We lived in a church parsonage that didn't allow pets, and by mid-morning the following day, we had been spotted taking the adult dogs out to the bathroom. It was no surprise when we received a call from the pastor, reminding us of the absolute no-pet policy. That was the first time I ever heard Jennifer's aforementioned sermon. The pastor was quickly humbled, but he still insisted that the animals had to go and the sooner the better. Although we couldn't keep them ourselves, by God's mercy, we found a good home for all of them within a week.

Since that time, we have rescued and adopted numerous dogs, cats, turtles, and birds. Each rescue has had its own challenges and has brought its own blessings. However, there is something in all of us animal-lovers that pushes us to be rescuers—to care about those creatures in need. What is this? I believe it is the reflection, pale though it is, of God who seeks the lost and rescues the perishing.

In the last chapter we learned of our "lostness" and the consequences that our rebellion against God brought into the world. After the expulsion of Adam and Eve from the garden, the state of humanity did not improve. In fact, things just got worse until, *"The LORD saw that the wickedness of man was great in the earth, and that every intention of the thoughts of his heart was only evil continually" (Genesis 6:5).* This indictment is terrible enough, but then we read some of the saddest words in human history, *"And the Lord regretted that he had made man on the earth, and it grieved him to his heart. So the Lord said, "I will blot out man whom I have created from the face of the land, man and animals and creeping things and birds of the heavens, for I am sorry that I have made them" (Genesis 6:6-7).* God was sorry that He made us. Our sinfulness was not a few wrong actions; it was the thoroughly darkened orientation of our hearts and minds.

Notice that God has the right, as our Creator and King, to judge and to punish us according to His pure and perfect standards. What stands out to me in this story is that the fate of all the animals is linked to ours. They suffer because of our sin. They die because we brought death into the world. What was the result of this clash between God's goodness and our wickedness? God's absolute commitment to what is right required him to punish those who held an absolute commitment to what is wrong. He did that by means of a cataclysmic worldwide flood. Almighty God, who made this planet out of the love and joy of his heart, wiped out virtually every single person and virtually every single animal in an act of righteous judgment upon the sinfulness of humanity. That great flood might seem extreme to us, but it was God being perfectly consistent with His holy Genesis, the book of origins, has taught us so much, including the fact that God is good and He made us to be good to each other and to the animals with which we share the earth. We also have learned that our sin always ends up hurting us, hurting others, and hurting all of creation. Our selfish and sinful ways always lead to death. Why did so many millions of animals have to die in the flood along with the sinful humans, who were ultimately responsible? **Since the beginning the *well being* of the animals has always been linked to the *well doing* of humanity.** As we obey God's command to care for the creation, the animals are blessed. When we disobey God's command, the animals suffer. God has created all of us to live in a complex web of inter-relatedness and mutual dependency. We may not want the responsibility, but God has laid it "squarely on our shoulders." It is easy to point our finger at the badness of others and all the while to ignore it in ourselves. Clearly, our hearts are just like those of our ancestors, self-seeking and rebellious. If that were the end of the story, it would be a hopeless tale indeed.

However, the narrative of the worldwide flood is not only about judgment of sin, but also about God's mercy and forgiveness. It is an amazing chronicle of rescue, like the one at the beginning of this chapter, only much bigger and better. God provided a way of rescue, and He delivered Noah and his family in a floating ark of safety. If God had only been merciful to and concerned about people, the ark could have been a small covered raft for a family of eight. Instead, it was an immense floating barn by which God saved not only a remnant of humanity, but also every kind of animal. In Genesis 6:19 God declares, *"Of every living thing of all flesh, you shall bring two of every sort into the ark to keep them alive with you.*

God made a way of escape. Before the rain ever started, God provided the long-lived humans of that day over one hundred years of opportunities to turn back to Him through the warnings and beckoning of Noah as he built the ark. When they did not turn back to God, He still extended mercy to Noah, Noah's family, and representatives of all animal life. You are here today because of God's merciful rescue. Your dog, cat, bird, horse, or ferret is here because of God's merciful rescue. The rainbow has been designated as a perpetual reminder of God's mercy and of His promise "to never again destroy" the world with flood.

The rescue of Noah saved humans and animals physically, but the root of our rebellion and its poisonous fruit remained firmly entrenched. However, God had another rescue plan. In fact, it was the greatest rescue plan of all time. It was a rescue that would save us completely, starting with the heart, working its way through our entire being, and eventually out to the restoration of all creation. God promises this rescue throughout the Old Testament. In one passage God uses the imagery of us as sheep and Himself as shepherd when He states, *"As a shepherd seeks out his flock when he is among his sheep that have been scattered, so will I seek out my sheep, and **I will rescue them** from all places where they have been scattered on a day of clouds and thick darkness" (Ezekiel 34:12).*

How was He going to do this? Was He going to throw us a rope and say, "now pull yourself up," or "here's a map, now find your way home," or "take this medicine for your ailment?" No. Our quandary was too great, our pit too deep, and our ailment fatal. We were now spiritually dead, and dead people don't need a rope, a map, or even medicine; they need a resurrection. They need a whole new life. They need to be born all over again. That's exactly what God's rescue plan accomplished.

How did He do this? God sent His one and only Son Jesus into this world on a divine mission of rescue. In other words, God came to us in the person of His Son. We couldn't work our way back to Him. We couldn't even contribute to our own rescue. We were dead in the water, and we needed a rescuer to jump in with us, to pull us out, and to resuscitate us. It all had to be done for us by another. In probably the most famous description of that rescue in the entire Bible, we read, *"For God so loved the world, that he gave his only Son, that whoever believes in him should not perish but have eternal life. For God did not send his Son into the world to condemn the world, but in order that the world might be saved through him" (John 3:16-17).* God's eternal Son took on human flesh in order to save the world. Certainly, humanity is in view in the word rendered "world" in this passage, and even though animals are unable to believe this message, they and the entire "world" benefit from our belief or suffer from our unbelief.

This message of Divine Rescue is the Gospel. According to the Bible, the Gospel of *who* Jesus is and *what* Jesus has done is of *first importance*. **The Gospel is the top priority for us to understand, receive, trust, and share with others**. As we share this message, God's Holy Spirit blesses it by bringing life to dead men and women. Addressing the Thessalonians, the Apostle Paul makes this point as he reminds them, *"Our gospel came to you not only in word, but also in power and in the Holy Spirit and with full conviction"* (1 Thessalonians 1:5).

Understanding who Jesus is begins with the Eternal Son leaving his place of visible power and authority at God the Father's right hand and taking on human flesh. He was born of the Virgin Mary some two thousand years ago in Bethlehem and was given the name Jesus. He lived a life just like ours, except with absolutely no rebellion against God. Not only was His life sinless, but also His life was permeated with total love and obedience to God and with perfect love for His neighbor.

To put a point on it, Jesus lived the life we were supposed to have lived. We have all fallen far short of the shining power and purpose for which we were created—but not Jesus. Even today when we read the New Testament accounts of Jesus' life, His brilliance shines like a beautiful and undeniable beacon of hope and inspiration. However, if showing us the way had been enough, God would have been satisfied with this perfect example of a human life, but life-examples don't really help corpses who have already drowned in a sea of their own sin. We needed a supernatural rebirth, but how could that happen with our sins remaining unpunished by a pure and perfect, heavenly Judge?

The Bible tells us, *"God shows his love for us in that while we were still sinners, Christ died for us" (Romans 5:8)*. The crux of Jesus' mission of rescue was not the manger at his birth, but the cross at His death. **Jesus died in our place. He took our sins upon His sinless shoulders. He received the full punishment for our sins from God the Father**. The Old Testament prophet Isaiah foretold this amazing act of sacrificial substitution some seven hundred years prior to the coming of Christ, when he said of Jesus, *"But he was wounded for our transgressions; he was crushed for our iniquities; upon him was the chastisement that brought us peace, and with his stripes we are healed. All we like sheep have gone astray; we have turned—every one—to his own way; and the LORD has laid on him the iniquity of us all" (Isaiah 53:5-6)*.

Jesus' death was not the final act in this dramatic rescue. On the third day after His death and burial, Jesus was bodily raised to life by God. This was God's divine seal of approval on Jesus' rescue mission. This was the first-fruit on the tree of resurrection that guarantees God's restoration of all things. Now God, through His Word and Spirit, calls on all people everywhere to turn from their sin and to trust Jesus Christ as their resurrected Savior and Lord.

Maybe you think that God has changed since the time of Noah or since the time of the New Testament? Maybe God has mellowed? Maybe we don't need to be rescued? Maybe He is less concerned with goodness, righteousness, and justice?

The answer to each of these questions is: NO. He is exactly the same, and He still does punish sin and threaten destruction for those who continue in their rebellion. Another day of judgment is coming upon the world, not with a flood but with fire, and all who ignore him will be judged. As in the days of Noah, God has provided an ark of deliverance and a ship of salvation. Our ark is His Son the Lord Jesus Christ, the Lamb of God, who received in himself the punishment for the sins of each and every person who believes in Him from *all* over the world and across *all* time.

In the first half of Romans 6:23 we read, *"For the wages of sin is death."* This tells us the bad news, but that bad news need not be the end of your story. That verse ends with the good news, *"But the free gift of God is eternal life in Christ Jesus our Lord."* There is an ark of safety open to all who will enter. Turn away from your foolish rebellion and ruinous self-love. Run into the God's ark of mercy by placing your faith and trust in Jesus Christ. Experiencing the forgiveness and new life provided for us by Jesus' death and resurrection. Flee to Jesus. He will save you. This is the Gospel for pet-lovers. This is the Gospel for everyone. This is the Good News for you. Do you believe? Do you trust the one and only divine rescuer, Jesus Christ? I pray that you do. I long for you to know the joy and peace of being rescued. Look to Jesus, your deliverer, and live! By the way, the next time you feel compelled to rescue that animal in danger, remember you are reflecting the image of your Creator, who sent His Son to rescue you and all who will believe.

Prayer of Placing Our Trust in Jesus Christ
O Lord God, Maker of Heaven and Earth,
We thank You for creating the animals, this beautiful planet, and us.
We are sorry we have rebelled against You and Your Word .
We know our rebellion has hurt us, has hurt the animals,
and has even hurt the entire planet.

Thank you for sending your Son Jesus to die in
our place for our sins.
Thank you that Jesus was raised from the dead to live forever
as our Savior and King.
We place our trust in the Lord Jesus Christ
and all that He has done to make us right with You.
Thank you that through Christ in the power of the Holy Spirit
we can know You, not only as our Creator, but as our
Father forever.
Through Jesus Christ our Lord we pray,

AMEN

Chapter Four

ADOPTED
Bringing an Animal into your
Heart and Home

But the poor man had nothing but one little ewe lamb, which he had
bought. And he brought it up, and it grew up with him and with his chil-
dren. It used to eat of his morsel and drink from his cup and lie in his arms,
and it was like a daughter to him.

(2 Samuel 12:3)

I grew up in a family that loved animals, but pets were meant to live outside. As adults my wife and I have been greatly blessed to share our home with various dogs and cats through the years. Even as I write these words on a cold and rainy fall day, I glance down from the loft to the sofa below and see our three dogs and newest cat curled up together. Two of the dogs and the cat were rescued on the side of the road. As I look at them, I realize they are a part of *my* family, and I am a part of *their* family. Rescuing them was great, but sharing life with them is even better. If you have ever brought an animal into your heart and home, you understand that the best word to describe this is "adoption."

I'm not talking about something legal, but about something relational: deeply bonded, profoundly meaningful, and very personal. As much as I might care for animals in general, I have a completely different level of connection and responsibility for those that are mine. They are family!

Remember our hound dogs, Rupert and Fiona? Rupert is black and white and loves to talk to you and box at you with his paws. He thinks "the sun rises and sets" on his sister Fiona. Fiona looks like a large beagle, or some have called her an English foxhound. She has the distinction of being the fastest-eating dog ever. We often laugh because her meal disappears before the bowl hits the ground. Sometimes when we look at them, Jennifer and I have fun trying to distinguish the various breeds in our Heinz 57 pooches. It doesn't really matter what they are; what matters is they are ours.

Nine years ago Jennifer was riding home from the grocery store and came upon two very young dogs in the middle of the road. Several cars had already stopped, and the dogs ran up to each door. No door opened, and the cars pulled away, leaving Jennifer alone with the two dogs. She managed to get them to a nearby parking lot. They were wild, dirty, and hungry. She called me and asked me to bring the horse trailer. When I arrived, I saw the dogs and thought, "Let's help these guys today and find their owners or a new home for them tomorrow." We already had eleven other animals at home: one dog, six cats, three horses, and one donkey. Surely, somebody else could take these. They did need to be rescued, but this was all we could do.

When we got them home, we realized they were completely unruly and unkempt. We couldn't even bring them near our other dog or into the house. While trying to figure out what to do, we left them in the empty horse stall in the barn. We checked throughout the community to see if any dogs were missing. Next, we called several rescue organizations trying to find a good home for them. Note to reader: Rescue groups are a great blessing, and we should all be extremely grateful for and supportive of the big-hearted people who serve in them!

Finally, we found a person who could take them temporarily, but they would have to live outside on a concrete pad until she found them a permanent home. That situation might have been better than I was imagining, but I couldn't get any peace about it. I knew it would be a significant commitment to bring these two into our lives: time in cleaning and treating them, effort in training them, and money for feeding and caring for them. Each time I tried to imagine their lives on that concrete pad or their being split up and sent to different homes of unknown quality, I could not stand it. If you are a regular rescuer, you understand that you can't keep every animal you rescue. However, I slowly realized that we could, with sacrifice, provide them with a better life than they could have elsewhere.

Jennifer and I were scheduled to go out of town the next day, and we were reluctant to add two "newbies" to the burden of animal care that her mother, who was looking after our crew, would have in our absence. Graciously, my mother- in-law offered to look after them. When we got home from our trip, the decision was made. We took those wild, dirty, mangy mutts into our lives. We adopted them. We brought them into our family. We bathed them. We nourished them. We named them. We slowly, but surely trained them, and we loved them. That is the story of how Rupert and Fiona became a part of the Brady bunch and are now sleeping soundly on the sofa.

The Bible doesn't say a lot about people having animals as pets. In the agrarian world of Bible times, animals were either wild or, if domesticated, served a specific function: sheep for wool, oxen for plowing, donkeys for transportation, and various others for food.

However, if we look just below the surface, we realize that many people in those days were personally bonded with their animals, just as we are today. One example is the parable Nathan the prophet told King David. That parable was directed at David's heart, intended to convict him of his sin with another man's wife. It told of a wicked rich man and a loving poor man. The poor man bought one little lamb and brought it home to be raised with his children. The affection and bond between the man and the lamb were so profound, *"It used to eat of his morsel and drink from his cup and lie in his arms, and it was like a daughter to him" (2 Samuel 12:3).*

Old Testament scholar Ronald Youngblood suggests that the verbs used in this story to describe the ewe lamb indicate it is prized as a genuine member of the poor man's family. This kind of closeness with an animal is one that any modern day pet-lover can truly understand. The story takes an awful turn when the greedy rich man steals and kills the poor man's lamb for food, even though he has flocks and herds of his own. He does not want to waste any of his own animals on a hospitality meal for a traveler, so he steals the poor man's precious little lamb.

If the thought of being closely bonded to an animal were unthinkable or repulsive in Bible times, King David would have rejected the story before it ever reached its powerful conclusion. Instead, the story slipped past David's emotional defenses, enabling him to see and feel the deep injustice of his sin because he could relate to caring deeply for an animal. Remember, he had grown up as a shepherd. He had spent weeks on end in the fields caring for the sheep, both night and day. He knew what it meant to let an animal into his heart. Nathan's animal story stirred up David's anger, causing him to pronounce judgment on the fictional sheep thief by saying, *"As the LORD lives, the man who has done this deserves to die" (2 Samuel 12:5).* Little did

David know *he* was the man because he had stolen Bathsheba from her husband, Uriah. Isn't it fascinating that the prophet Nathan chose a story of love between a man and an animal to reach the hardened heart of his king? This is powerful evidence that people were more bonded with animals in biblical times than we might have imagined.

If you are skeptical about people in the Bible being bonded with animals, I offer one more consideration. Simply, people in those days had much more regular contact with animals than the majority of us do today. Undoubtedly, some of those animals won a special place in the hearts and homes of their owners. Even though this is not precisely the same as our "pets" today, I believe there are enough similarities to warrant the analogies in this chapter.

One objection to the idea of people caring about animals in biblical times is the horror of animal sacrifice. We might think this is an indication of animals being less valued than they are now. **Actually, animal sacrifices were just as horrible to them as they are to us; that's the point!** The revulsion of having to kill an innocent animal was meant to show the depths of the consequences of sin. Remember, our *well doing* is inextricably linked to the *well being* of all creation, particularly other living creatures such as the animals. Animal sacrifices were costly: financially, physically, emotionally, and spiritually. Granted, people may have grown numb to its horror, but that is not because the horror wasn't there. Slitting the throat of a lamb from ear to ear is bloody and awful in any generation! Those sacrifices were intended to humble people and to break their hearts over the wickedness of their sins, showing them the painful price God's justice demands in order for sins to be covered. One indication that sacrificing the Passover Lamb was meant to be emotionally wrenching is contained in the following instructions God gave to Moses:

*Tell all the congregation of Israel that **on the tenth day*** *of this month every man shall take a lamb according to their fathers' houses, a lamb for a household... Your lamb shall be without blemish, a male a year old.... and **you shall keep it until the fourteenth day*** *of this month, when the whole assembly of the congregation of Israel **shall kill their lambs*** *at twilight. (Exodus 12:3-6)*

These Passover lambs were no anonymous sheep slaughtered in an impersonal way by strangers. One spotless year-old lamb was taken into each household four days prior to its being sacrificed. Why? Among other things, it is so that the lamb would be personally known and cared for by the entire family. Can you imagine how much more moving this would be, especially to the children? Tears would have been streaming down faces as the family lamb was slain. Yes, the blood of that lamb would protect them, but what a heart-wrenching price!

Before we arrogantly think ourselves more tender-hearted than our Old Testament forbearers, consider how many times animals have filled our tables and our stomachs without a passing thought of what that means. We don't even pause to consider that an animal had to die in order for us to have that meal. We have no humility over the life given for us; no gratitude for the sacrifice made on our behalf; and no concern over the way the animal was raised or slaughtered. Maybe we are not as tenderhearted as we think.

That's where the God's glorious gospel comes into view. Christians continue to believe that our many sins need to be forgiven. God uses the sacrificial system of the Old Testament to prepare us for the supreme and final sacrifice for sin. That sacrifice on our behalf is His Son, Jesus Christ! When John the Baptist saw Jesus, he did not say, "Behold, the greatest teacher who has come to take away our ignorance" or "Behold, the greatest revolutionary who has come to create the perfect government," rather, he solemnly declares, *"Behold, the Lamb of God who takes away the sin of the world" (John 1:29).*

How are we, who continue in a pattern of repeated sins, made right with God without repeated sacrifices? The Bible explains:

> *And every priest stands daily at his service, offering repeatedly the same sacrifices, which can never take away sins. But when Christ had offered for all time a single sacrifice for sins, he sat down at the right hand of God, waiting from that time until his enemies should be made a footstool for his feet. For by a single offering he has perfected for all time those who are being sanctified. (Hebrews 10:11-14)*

Jesus is the once-for-all perfect sacrifice. No more sacrifices are needed! If you will trust Him, you can know that your sins are forgiven: fully, freely, and forever. We don't sacrifice our animals because Jesus has been sacrificed for us, and by His sacrifice we are saved. The sacrifice of Jesus, the Lamb of God, will forever remain the center of the praises of God's people, on earth and in heaven. We see this in the song of the ones rescued from every corner of the earth praising the Lamb, *"Worthy are you to take the scroll and to open its seals, for you were slain, and by your blood you ransomed people for God from every tribe and language and people and nation" (Revelation 5:9).*

In answer to the question of whether some people in the Bible were close to their animals, I would say: YES. Animals were loved and appreciated then as now. At least some of them were brought into the hearts and homes of people. Animals were central to their world, and the Bible is filled with them. These facts prepare us for taking the next step in our examination of the Gospel for pet-lovers.

The Bible teaches that every person rescued by God is made a part of His family. We are not only pulled from the sea of sinfulness to be given a new life, but we are also given a new family. God our Creator is now God our Father. All of those rescued by Him are our brothers and sisters. The Bible says, *"But to all who did receive him, who believed in his name, he gave the right to become children of God, who were born, not believed in his name, He gave the right to become children of God, who were born, not of blood nor of the will of the flesh nor of the will of man, but of God" (John 1:12-13)*. If you have received your rescuer, Jesus Christ, and believe in who He is and what He has done on your behalf, He gives you the right to become a child of God.

The Bible makes this point explicit when it says, *"But when the fullness of time had come, God sent forth his Son, born of woman, born under the law, to redeem those who were under the law, **so that we might receive adoption as sons**. And because you are sons, God has sent the Spirit of his Son into our hearts, crying, 'Abba! Father!'" (Galatians 4:4-6)*. Did you notice the purpose statement in the middle of the verses quoted above? It provides the answer to why Jesus came and what His redemption (purchasing the freedom of slaves) was intended to do. What is that purpose? It is so that we might receive adoption as sons. In God's family, women and men receive an equal adoption with full rights to a full inheritance. Isn't the Gospel amazing?

Adoption, of all the biblical realities related to our rescue, strikes the deepest emotional chord in my heart. I can understand God's rescue and adoption more clearly through the animals we have rescued and adopted. In my memory, I can see their dirty faces staring up at me and asking, "What now? You rescued me, but what now?" If they only knew that they were going to be a part of our family. Their welfare is our concern. We are committed to them. We will make our way together through life. And isn't life together, even with all its challenges, much better than life alone?

This "life of togetherness" is precisely the kind of life that God the Father provides for us. We aren't the only ones He has rescued. We have numerous brothers and sisters that have also been rescued and brought into His family. He designed it so that we would share life together. This group of rescued or called out ones is *the church*. The Bible says that, *"You are no longer strangers and aliens, but you are fellow citizens with the saints and members of the household of God"* (Ephesians 2:19). **One of God's purposes in salvation is to give us a new family—*His!*** The church is not a building, but a people. It is not an organization, but a family. It is a family brought and kept together by its common faith in Jesus Christ. It is a family called to live, work, and worship together. It is a family made up of people from all over the world and across all time. It is a family of men and women who come from a vast diversity of ethnicities, languages, and cultures, and yet they are brothers and sisters forever.

I know many people who have trusted Christ and believe He has rescued and adopted them into God's family, but they want no part of the church. They call the church "organized religion" and deliberately avoid it as unnecessary or even unhelpful. They would agree with the Christian who joked, "To live with the saints above, oh that will be glory, but to live with the saints below, now that's a different story."

I understand the sentiment. I have been a pastor for over twenty-five years and have been a part of churches my entire life. I have seen the deep ugliness that can go on in churches. I have seen hypocrisy in a number of professing Christians. I've seen believers, especially myself, fail to live up to the virtues of the faith. Despite the presence of hypocrisy and disappointments, we must never forsake this simple truth—we were rescued to become a family. The Bible knows nothing of believers who deliberately choose to live their lives solo. We are intended to live out the Christian life with brothers and sisters. Bearing each other's burdens. Praying for each other. Teaching each other. Correcting each other. All in the Spirit of love. Amazingly, the Father has adopted us into *His* family. We are not yet a perfect family, but we are a family in the process of being made perfect by our perfect Savior. His Spirit now lives in us, *"Crying Abba! Father!"* (Romans 8:16). If you are not a part of a local fellowship of believers, prayerfully follow Christ into a church that honors Him, His Word, and His Gospel.

Think about the animals you have brought into your heart and home. In them you have a glimmer of the beauty of spiritual adoption into the family of God. God's family is one that will have frustrations but one that will provide much strength and encouragement for the journey to the Father's House. Through the Gospel of Jesus Christ, God is not merely our Creator or Judge but has become our Father. All who believe are God's children. We have a myriad of brothers and sisters. **We are *family*!**

Rupert and Fiona

Fiona, Ari and Rupert in the snow

The author with Rupert and Fiona

Jennifer and Fiona

Rupert playing

Chapter Five

TRAINED
Making Our Pets into Good Family Members

For the moment all discipline seems painful rather than pleasant, but later it
yields the peaceful fruit of righteousness to those who have been trained by it.
(Hebrews 12:11)

We all know how upsetting undisciplined pets can be. They bark, bite, sniff, jump, chew, pee, pooh, and pull whenever and wherever they want. They rarely listen. They embarrass us in public or when friends come over to visit. Living with them becomes more of a burden than a blessing. Those cute puppies or kittens have become tyrants. The behavior that was once comical has become a serious problem. We rescued them. We adopted them into our family. Now why are they acting so badly? They need to be trained. We gladly brought them into our families, just as they were, but not to leave them that way. We want them to grow up, behave well, and be all-around good family members. This goal requires an intentional, daily growth process to help them become the best pets possible. In the end, this will make both them and us happier.

As soon as I open this can of worms, a few of my "problem children" come to mind. I must admit, when it comes to training, "my talk is better than my walk." I have not been consistent in my efforts to discipline them. My dogs pull on their leases when I walk them, but they don't pull when my wife walks them. Hum? I wonder where doth the problem lie? We have a longhaired cat, Prince William, who tries to kill us when we are combing out the burrs in his coat. Let's not forget the donkey. Oh, the donkey. Always the donkey.

Burrito has spent the past decade finding ways to get into trouble. Right now as I look out the window, I see Burrito happily munching grass in our front yard (he's not supposed to be there). Somehow, he mysteriously escaped the pasture, leaving his horse friend behind. The fence works just fine to keep the horse in but not "Houdini donkey." Burrito does whatever he wants, whenever he wants. Listening to us is not very high on his list of priorities. On one occasion, we were trying to load him onto the horse trailer. He needed to visit the vet for a check-up, but he would have none of it. We attempted everything. We pushed. We pulled. We bribed. We yelled, but to no avail. He was not getting on that trailer. Finally, in exasperation Jennifer shouted, "Burrito, in the name of Jesus, get on that trailer!" To my utter amazement that donkey shot onto the trailer like a bolt of lightning, forcing me to dive out of the way to avoid getting run over. Jennifer and I stood in stunned silence for a long moment, looked at each other, and exclaimed, "Why didn't we think of that before!" As pet owners, we all have stories of animal disobedience that make us chuckle, but we know that a constant pattern of undisciplined behavior is unacceptable. Everyone is better off when our pets are well trained.

We began to learn this lesson with our second dog, Fionn Connal. Fionn was a brindled Irish wolfhound. We first laid eyes on him as a puppy in a yard filled with Wolfhounds. If you've never met an Irish wolfhound, you have not yet lived. They are among the most unique looking creatures in the dog world. Stepping into that yard was like entering a scene from Jurassic Park. Numerous gigantic hounds lounged lazily in the Oklahoma sun. Then we saw him. Our little puppy weighed around eighteen pounds and had a tummy that dragged the ground. We saw that the adults were really large, but we could not fully prepare ourselves for what lay ahead.

We brought Fionn back to Fort Worth, Texas, where we were living at the time. There he met our first dog, a five-pound Yorkshire terrier named Indy, whom we had hardly trained at all. We realized Fionn was going to be too large *not* to train. If we didn't train him and train him fast, he would soon be uncontrollable. We set about a daily process of training him to walk on a leash, heel, sit, come, and be a solid citizen. We are glad we did because that puppy of eighteen pounds grew and grew and grew. We would go to bed at night and wake up the next day with a larger Fionn. Also, he grew in a curious way. Some days he would have long legs with a small body, and other days he would have a huge body and short legs. When he finished growing, he weighed over 165 pounds, and the top of his back measured 36 inches from the ground. When I placed his front paws on my shoulders, his head was more than seven feet above the ground! He was a behemoth in size and looked ferocious, but he was one of the gentlest spirits I've ever known.

As we trained him, we learned several invaluable lessons: start young, be clear, be consistent, be firm (but not harsh), make the wrong behavior uncomfortable, and reward the right behavior. Fionn made a lot of progress in obedience, and I think he wanted to please us, but to the end nothing motivated him like a good dog biscuit. Although Irish wolfhounds are not known for entering official obedience trials, Fionn completed his Companion Dog (CD) certification. Even though Fionn was large and strong, he was a great family member. Eventually, he was able to go into nursing homes as a Pet-Therapy Dog. Everyone loved him, and he loved them in return. Why was he so special? Unquestionably, his nature was unique, but his training was vital to his usefulness.

In the same way, Christians need to be trained. We come into the family of God and are not particularly good family members until we've been taught. The process of being trained is *discipleship*, and the resulting growth is *sanctification*. Christian disciples are students of Christ. We learn from Him what is true, and we learn from Him how to live.

In his final instructions to his disciples, Jesus commissions them to make disciples of others. He says, *"Go therefore and make disciples of all nations, baptizing them in the name of the Father and of the Son and of the Holy Spirit, teaching them to observe all that I have commanded you. And behold, I am with you always, to the end of the age"* (Matthew 28:19-20). The rescue and adoption of sinners are not the totality of Christ's work. He also *transforms* those he rescues. First, the journey begins as we place our trust in Him. Second, we are publically identified as his disciples by our baptism in the name of the Father, the Son, and the Holy Spirit. Third, our growth continues each day as we are taught to obey

Him in all things. Finally, we are reminded that never once do we walk or work alone. He is with us every step of the way to the end of the world.

The final shape, into which we are being transformed, is not vague or ill defined. **We are being transformed into the image of Jesus.** Paul puts forth this reality, *"For those whom he foreknew he also predestined **to be conformed to the image of his Son**, in order that he might be the firstborn among many brothers" (Romans 8:29).* Becoming like Christ is the goal. He is the perfect one, and we are being made like Him. As God empowers this renovation, we begin to think more like Jesus, feel more like Jesus, and live more like Jesus. However, it does not happen automatically. We must make an effort toward this goal day after day. When we fail, we ask God for forgiveness. We never lose hope, knowing that what God starts, God finishes. He is the Faithful Trainer who will see us through until we are fully conformed to the image of Jesus Christ.

How do we get started in this process? My favorite verse in the Bible says, *"And we all, with unveiled face, beholding the glory of the Lord, are being transformed into the same image from one degree of glory to another. For this comes from the Lord who is the Spirit" (2 Corinthians 3:18).* We begin by fixing our eyes on Jesus! As we keep our gaze set on him, we are transformed (metamorphosed) to be like Him. Slowly but surely, we begin to resemble him.

So how do we see Jesus? Is it some sort of vision, or feeling, or imagination that we muster? No. We see Christ in and through the Bible. It is our trustworthy guide for getting to know Jesus. 2 Timothy 3:16-17 declares, *"All Scripture is breathed out by God and profitable for teaching, for reproof, for correction, and for training in righteousness, that the man of God may be competent, equipped for every good work.*" In the Scriptures, we get a clear and compelling picture of who Jesus is, and of what he taught and did. From this biblical portrait we learn what we are to believe and how we are to live.

The biblical way of seeing is through words, not physical images. Therefore, listening is the essential first ingredient in all discipleship. We are called to listen carefully to the voice of our Master. This priority of learning to listen is exactly the same for our pets. We can't train them to do anything until we train them to listen. Likewise, God will not train us until we learn to listen. Jesus highlights the importance of hearing his voice by using animal imagery. In John 10:4-5 he likens himself to a shepherd and his disciples to sheep, *"and the sheep follow him, for they know his voice. A stranger they will not follow, but they will flee from him, for they do not know the voice of strangers."* Do you know the shepherd's voice?

As we fix our eyes on Jesus Christ, the author and the perfecter of our faith, we begin to see our sin: wrong attitudes, ideas, desires, and behaviors that belong to our old life. We are called to strip off each and every one of these and to keep fighting against them until our final breath. The Apostle Paul says, *"Put to death therefore what is earthly in you: sexual immorality, impurity, passion, evil desire, and covetousness, which is idolatry" (Colossians 3:5).* We don't obey this command in order *to become* a part of the family of God. We obey this command because we are grateful and secure in the reality that we *already belong* to God's family. We are motivated by gratitude for the amazing grace God has extended to us. However, this growth in Christ-likeness is not only a "putting off of the bad," but also a "putting on of the good." Paul continues a few verses later, *"Put on then, as God's chosen ones, holy and beloved, compassionate hearts, kindness, humility, meekness, and patience, bearing with one another and, if one has a complaint against another, forgiving each other; as the Lord has forgiven you, so you also must forgive" (Colossians 3:12-13).* We put on all these virtues in an environment of forgiveness. Notice the standard we are called to use in granting forgiveness, *"Forgiving each other; as the Lord has forgiven you."* We *give* and *forgive* others as Christ has *given* and *forgiven* us. We are now called to live like Jesus in the power of being united to Him by faith.

At the beginning of the chapter, we quoted a verse from Hebrews 12:11, *"For the moment all discipline seems painful rather than pleasant, but later it yields the peaceful fruit of righteousness to those who have been trained by it."* All discipline is painful while we are experiencing it, but later that same discipline brings forth a bumper-crop of great benefits. The contemporary motto that best expresses this training is, "no pain, no gain."

The same thing applies to our animals. The more we give them consistent training and discipline, the better family members they will become. Remember, disciples are those who undergo discipline. **The Christian's motto for growth is, "No discipline, No disciple."** Therefore, the Christian life is about growth in becoming more and more like Christ. That growth is a result of the gracious work of God's Holy Spirit in us, empowering us to put forth more and more effort each day in the fight against sin and for the fullness of goodness in our lives. The Bible urges us to:

Make every effort to supplement your faith with virtue, and virtue with knowledge, and knowledge with self-control, and self-control with steadfastness, and steadfastness with godliness, and godliness with brotherly affection, and brotherly affection with love. For if these qualities are yours and are increasing, they keep you from being ineffective or unfruitful in the knowledge of our Lord Jesus Christ. (2 Peter 1:5-8)

There are other means that God gives us to grow, and we learn about all of them from His Word. Don't squander your rescue; become a good family member. Make every effort toward that goal — starting today!

If you aren't familiar with the Bible, you could begin by reading the Gospel according to Mark. It is the shortest of the four gospels and will serve as a great introduction to the life and teachings of Jesus Christ. We also have a list of practical suggestions and recommended books addressing spiritual growth on the website www. livinginthevertical.com.

We have seen the numerous parallels between our growth in obedience and the growth in obedience of our animals. Most pet-owners are satisfied with modest improvements in their animal's behavior. Not so with God. He does not merely want external conformity to His rules. He desires a complete and total transformation that starts in the heart and mind and works its way out into our behavior. Paul praises God for this extreme make-over, *"But thanks be to God, that you who were once slaves of sin **have become obedient from the heart** to the standard of teaching to which you were committed, and,* *having been set free from sin, have become slaves of righteousness"* *(Romans 6:17-18).* If training is necessary for our animals in order for them to become good members of our family, how much more necessary training must be in order for us to become good members of God's family.

Chapter Six

CARED FOR
Taking Care of the Animals God has Entrusted to Us

The godly care for their animals…
(Proverbs 12:10a, NLT)

I care not for a man's religion whose dog and cat are not the better for it.
Abraham Lincoln

Seeing an animal abused or neglected gets my blood boiling! Recently on a rainy afternoon, I was taking the trash to our local recycling center. I saw a mother dog and her puppy hiding underneath one of the trailers. I asked the man in charge about them, and he said they had been there all day. On closer examination, I realized the mother dog was dragging a large chain that she had obviously pulled with her from wherever she had been tied. She was very skittish and did not like it when I got close. The puppy was friendlier, but it was obvious they were scared, hungry, and wet. The supervisor found a name and number on the dog's collar. I left the dogs and went home, hoping to contact their owner. We called the number, but no one answered. By doing a reverse search on the number, we got the address. We headed back to the dogs at the recycling center, fed them, put them in our vehicle, and took them back to their home.

When we arrived at the address, we were overwhelmed by what we found. No one was home as we entered the yard, which was filled with piles of junk and rusting old cars sitting on blocks. The level of squalor was appalling. There were puppies running everywhere, an adult male tied with a chain, and several other dogs in the back of the yard. The nearly empty water bowl was filled with slime. My blood pressure was rising. How could anybody treat animals like this?

After making sure every dog on the property was well fed, we headed off to contact the authorities. At first we found very little help. The only advice we were given was to be careful not to get arrested for trespassing. Eventually, we found a rescue group who was willing to handle the situation. That group contacted the owner, whose excuse was that he worked long hours and could not look after his animals any better. We went back the next day and fed them again, but we knew this situation was beyond our ability to resolve. We wanted to do more, but what? The rescue group was scheduled to come that afternoon. Maybe, they could do something we could not. Finally, at the end of the day, we had to leave it to the professionals, but I still get sick when I think about the life those poor creatures had to endure. So much of the quality of an animal's life depends upon the character of its owner. That is why we see such horrible neglect and abuse all around us.

One of the most beloved passages in the Bible is an animal bragging about its owner. The animal goes to unforgettable poetic heights in singing the praises of the one who cares for him. What passage of

Scripture is that? Of course, it is the twenty-third Psalm. Let's refresh our memories of this most beautiful song by re-reading it with an eye to see its animal imagery:

> *The LORD is my shepherd; I shall not want.*
> *He makes me lie down in green pastures.*
> *He leads me beside still waters.*
> *He restores my soul. He leads me in paths of righteousness*
> *for his name's sake.*
> *Even though I walk through the valley of the shadow of death,*
> *I will fear no evil, for you are with me;*
> *your rod and your staff, they comfort me.*
> *You prepare a table before me in the presence of my enemies;*
> *You anoint my head with oil; my cup overflows.*
> *Surely goodness and mercy shall follow me all the days of my life,*
> *and I shall dwell in the house of the LORD forever.*
> *(Psalm 23:1-6)*

This psalm gives us a portrait of how God cares for us and of how we should care for those in our charge. The shepherd in the psalm establishes a sense of belonging between himself and the sheep. He feeds and waters the sheep. He picks them up when they are down. He leads them well by choosing good paths. He protects them in dark and dangerous situations. When they are hurt, he nurses their wounds, and he stays with the sheep until they are safely home. The response of the sheep to that kind of shepherd is a deep sense of security and happiness.

The element of "belonging" is the fundamental aspect of the relationship between sheep and shepherd. The sheep know to which shepherd they belong. The shepherd is committed to them, and they feel the power of that bond. That bond takes place when you adopt a particular animal as your own. As much as you may love animals in general, you have a unique responsibility for those that belong to you. We don't feed and look after every animal we see, only those that belong to us. That's why the moment of committing to an animal is so significant. It changes the relationship forever. Commitments are powerful and are described throughout the Bible using the word "covenant." God made a covenant with believers to bring them *into* and to keep them *in* a right relationship with Him. The covenantal name for God in the Bible is LORD, which is a modest and cautious way to represent the Divine Name YHWH (transliterated "Yahweh" or in the past "Jehovah"). That is the name David uses for God in the opening line of the twenty-third Psalm. How did God become LORD to the sheep in the Psalm? Let's find out.

The sense of belonging is established as the psalm begins, *"The LORD is my shepherd, I shall not want."* The sheep "speaking" wants everybody to know who his shepherd is (Remember, the author of this song was David, who had himself been a shepherd). This sheep had a great life because its master was so good. In the words of Phillip Keller in his excellent little book, A Shepherd Looks at Psalm 23, *"The lot in life of any particular sheep depended on the type of man who owned it."* So how does the relationship between sheep and shepherd begin?

The beginning of our relationship with the Shepherd is actually described in the prior Psalm. Psalm 22 is amazing prophetic account of the crucifixion of Jesus written 1,000 years before it happened. The last verse declares, *"He has done it"* or *"He has fulfilled it."* Immediately we ask, "Who has done what?" **The answer is Jesus**

has done it. He has paid the debt of our sin. The same truth is recorded in John 19:30 when Jesus cries out from the cross, *"It is finished!"* **The Gospel is always about what God has done for us and not about what we do for God.** Most religions and philosophies cry out, "Do!" Christ cries out, "Done!" As we "rest" in who Christ is and what Christ has done to reconcile us to God, His benefits begin to flow to us. The Holy Spirit applies to the individual believer the redemption that Christ accomplished. Therefore, to say that the LORD is our shepherd is to say we trust that Jesus died for our sins. We trust He did everything we need in order to make us right with God. He has graciously opened the door to never-ending relationship. God has become our covenantal LORD. By faith, we enter into an unbreakable, unalterable, unending relationship of love between sheep and shepherd. **In the spiritual realm God establishes "our belonging to Him" and "His belonging to us." We reflect that pattern in our relationship with our animals.**

Caring begins with your pets' knowing they belong to you and you belong to them. The shepherd also cares for the sheep by feeding and watering it well. The sheep is made to lie down in green grass, is led by still waters, and has a table prepared for it. Its cup overflows! The shepherd knows what nutrition the sheep needs to thrive and provides it. The food is species appropriate, as in "grass for sheep." The food is excellent quality as evidenced by its green color. The animal doesn't feel hurried or unprotected while eating because it is watched over by the shepherd. When satisfied, it is made to lie down and take a nap. Now that is an awesome shepherd! In fact, I could use a right about now. How about you? King David says the same earlier in Psalm 4:8, *"In peace I will both lie down and sleep; alone, O LORD, make me dwell in safety."* **The Gospel is ab** "the rest" one gains when he or she realizes that God, in Jesus Christ, has provided all we need to be right with Him.

The shepherd is thoughtful in how he waters the sheep. Notice that the psalm says the shepherd leads the sheep by "still waters." This suggests several factors that the shepherd considered in selecting where to water the sheep. The phrase "still waters" indicates a slow moving stream that is safe, but not stagnant. The water is clean, pure, and not dangerous. Phillip Keller points out, "When sheep are thirsty they become restless and set out in search of water to satisfy their thirst. If not led to the good supplies of clean, pure water, they will often end up drinking from the polluted pot holes where they pick up internal parasites and nematodes, liver flukes or other disease germs" (A Shepherd Looks at the Psalm 23, Phillip Keller, Pg. 50).

Bad and careless shepherds do not take care watering their animals and let them drink polluted water or water that is dangerously swift. However, the LORD's sheep are blessed because He leads them to pristine streams of living water. Jesus says, *"If anyone thirsts, let him come to me and drink. Whoever believes in me, as the Scripture has said, 'Out of his heart will flow rivers of living water'"* (John 7:37-38).

Furthermore, the shepherd encourages the sheep. When the psalm says he restores the soul of the sheep, it means he gently picks the sheep up when it falls and puts it back on its feet. Sheep often find a comfortable place to lie down in a dip and become cast. Remember, being cast means being stuck upside down. A cast sheep will bloat and die if they stay upside down, but the good shepherd comes and restores them. We pet-owners do this for our animals by being gentle and kind to them. God does this for us when we are discouraged by comforting and strengthening us.

Additionally, the sheep says of the shepherd, *"He leads me in paths of righteousness for His name's sake."* A good shepherd leads the sheep in good paths. The shepherd teaches us right from wrong. We are trained. We are set on a different path that will ultimately lead us home. Yes, the path will not always be easy, but it is headed in the right direction. Day by day the shepherd leads us, *"To put on the new self, created after the likeness of God in true righteousness and holiness" (Ephesians 4:24).* As we follow Jesus, we will begin to think, feel, and act more like Him. Does that mean that the Christian life will be one of stepping higher and higher each day on a straight path?

We only need to look at the next line in the psalm to find the answer, *"Even though, I walk through the valley of the shadow of death I will fear no evil for you are with me, your rod and staff they comfort me."* This sheep feels safe. It is cared for because the shepherd is there with it. The shepherd is looking out for it and protecting it. Whenever Jennifer and I are walking our dogs and there is a sudden noise, they first look to us. If we are scared, they are scared. If we're calm, it calms them. Animals, who know they can rely on their owners, are confident in dark and dangerous situations. They know their owner is right there with them and is worthy of their trust.

Jesus promises us he will always be right beside us in the person of the Holy Spirit. In John 14:16-17 Jesus tells His disciples, *"I will ask the Father, and he will give you another Helper, to be with you forever, even the Spirit of truth, whom the world cannot receive, because it neither sees him nor knows him. You know him, for he dwells with you and will be in you."* That's how Jesus can say that He is always with us. The word rendered *"Helper"* in the above verse is expressed idiomatically in various tribal languages as, *"the one who mothers us"* or *"the one who falls down beside us."* It is an individual, who upon finding a person collapsed along the road, kneels down beside the victim to care for his needs and carries him to safety. Does your pet know you will be there for them through green pastures and dark valleys?

When the sheep is injured, the shepherd cares for it by anointing its head with oil. This oil was part salve, part fly repellent. As pet owners, we know how much time, money, and effort is spent looking after the physical ailments of our animals. They get cut, have upset stomachs, are bitten by bugs, and fall prey to every kind of physical ailment imaginable. A good owner does not ignore those ailments but lovingly treats each and every one of them. God is the same with us. He knows all our bumps, bruises, and illnesses; He heals, comforts, and gives guidance through them all. **Our good shepherd is also our great physician.** Let us, *"Cast all our cares on Him because He cares for us" (1 Peter 5:7).*

The culmination of this psalm is the sheep's arrival home. We learn from the good shepherd to stay with the sheep to the end. The shepherd is loyal to journey's end. It is not always possible for us frail and feeble humans to keep every pet we own until their final breath, but that should be our goal. If we take them in, we should keep them to the end. Even though that may not be the case for all of our animals, it is true for the sheep in the twenty-third psalm that declares, *"and I shall dwell in the house of the LORD forever."* Do you notice the contentedness of this sheep? It is really happy because it has a great shepherd. In fact, that sense of contentment was expressed by the sheep at the beginning of the psalm when it said, *"I shall not want,"* or *"I'll never lack anything I need because I'm in good hands."*

In summary, the sheep says it is well fed, well led, well protected, and well cared for in every way and throughout every circumstance of life. This sheep is fed ample amounts of green grass and watered by pure, clean streams. It is picked up when knocked down. It is always led in good paths, and when it does enter dark and dangerous valleys, the shepherd doesn't abandon it. When the sheep is injured, healing oil is administered to the wound. Its water bowl is always running over. Every kind of good blessing is provided, propelling the sheep along the road home. **This "talking" sheep is contented and well cared for, all being a reflection of the amazing quality and character of its shepherd.**

Later in the Old Testament God decries the bad shepherding practices of the leaders of His people when He says:

> *Ah, shepherds of Israel who have been feeding yourselves! Should not shepherds feed the sheep? You eat the fat, you clothe yourselves with the wool, you slaughter the fat ones, but you do not feed the sheep. The weak you have not strengthened, the sick you have not healed, the injured you have not bound up, the strayed you have not brought back, the lost you have not sought, and with force and harshness you have ruled them. (Ezekiel 34:2-4)*

These self-centered shepherds used the sheep for their own purposes but did not have genuine care for the sheep. Notice the things these shepherds should have been doing with a gentle, loving spirit: feeding, strengthening, healing, and rescuing. The reality is they are more concerned about themselves than their animals. We see the same thing today with people that are animal-*users* rather than animal-*lovers*.

If your animals could speak, what would they say about the quality of care they have received from you? Would they brag or lament? Do we reflect to our animals the care we ourselves have received from our Heavenly Father? Whatever we do, even taking care of our animals, we are to do it for the glory of God. Would your animal say you feed it well? Do you make sure to give it the most nutritious, species-appropriate food you can afford? Do you ever think about the quality of what you are feeding? We wonder why our animals are sick, overweight, uncomfortable, and lethargic. They are just like us. They need good food and good exercise. I'm *not* recommending a particular diet, but *I am* recommending you research healthy diets for your animal. If you look for the truth, you will find it. Jennifer and I have used various diets through the years, but over the past decade we have been feeding a raw diet to our cats and dogs. We have been amazed with the vitality they have experienced as a result. Feeding a raw diet is labor intensive, and it can cost more than a pre-packaged diet. If you are interested in learning more, go to www.livinginthevertical.com (where you will find additional information and resources for healthy pet nutrition).

If you are committed to feeding a store-bought food, make sure you read the ingredient labels. When you compare several brands you will quickly see that not all foods are created equal. Many of them have very little nutritional value and will lead to diminished health for your beloved pet. As we have spent more money on food, we have spent less on veterinary care. If an animal is worth having, they are worth taking care of. The first part of Proverbs 12:10 plainly states, *"The godly care for their animals."* As God has cared for us, so we are called to care for those entrusted to us.

How does this theme of shepherding relate to the Gospel? Jesus makes the connection when he tells us that He is The Good Shepherd of the sheep. He contrasts himself with those wicked users of the sheep when He says, *"The thief comes only to steal and kill and destroy. I came that they may have life and have it abundantly. I am the good shepherd. The good shepherd lays down his life for the sheep" (John 10:10-11).* **Jesus came on a rescue mission to seek and to save all of His lost sheep, and He did it by laying down His life for them.**

Can you say that Jesus is your shepherd? If He is, then you are blessed with every spiritual blessing, and you will be well led. One hymn writer, Dorothy Thrupp, beautifully expresses what we have been discussing when she writes:

> *Savior, like a shepherd lead us*
> *Much we need Thy tender care*
> *In Thy pleasant pastures feed us*
> *For our use Thy folds prepare*
> *Blessed Jesus, blessed Jesus*
> *Thou hast bought us, Thine we are*

I pray that the Good Shepherd has found you. I pray that He is guiding your life. He will never lead you astray. All you need He will provide. He is the model of perfect caring for those entrusted to Him. Look to Him, and he will equip you to care for your husband, wife, children, friends, and even your animals. I pray God will do for you what is stated in this beautiful blessing from the Bible, *"Now may the God of peace who brought again from the dead our Lord Jesus, the great shepherd of the sheep, by the blood of the eternal covenant, **equip you with everything good that you may do his will**, working in us that which is pleasing in his sight, through Jesus Christ, to whom be glory forever and ever" (Hebrews 13:20-21),*

Chapter Seven

LOVED
The Priority of Love in All that We Are and Do

We love because he first loved us.
(1 John 4:19)

Love anything and your heart will be wrung and possibly broken. If you want to make sure of keeping it intact you must give it to no one, not even an animal. Wrap it carefully round with hobbies and little luxuries; avoid all entanglements. Lock it up safe in the casket or coffin of your selfishness. But in that casket—safe, dark, motionless, airless—it will change. It will not be broken; it will become unbreakable, impenetrable, and irredeemable. To love is to be vulnerable.
C.S. Lewis, <u>The Four Loves</u>

Who was your first pet? Mine was a puppy named Bozo. When I was five or six, I picked him out of a litter and was thrilled to have my very own dog. Sure, we had several other family dogs, but this was different; Bozo was mine. It was love at first sight. One day, soon after getting him, I came home to find that he was gone. I looked everywhere, but he just wasn't there. Some friends had come by earlier, and they really liked Bozo so my Dad gave him to them. I was crushed. Dad was truly sorry because he had not realized how attached I was. He offered to get me another puppy, but I would have nothing to do with that. My heart had been broken. It was a few years later before I would allow myself to become attached to another animal. Why did losing Bozo hurt so badly? In the words of C.S. Lewis, "To love is to be vulnerable."

My second dog's name was Happy. He was a medium-sized mixed breed with lots of curly black hair. I got him at the pound when I was about thirteen years old. My parents were Christian missionaries, and we lived in Central America, but that year we were living in the USA with my aunt in Landrum, South Carolina. Happy was a great companion from the beginning. He loved me, and I loved him. I enjoyed basketball, and he would stay with me as long as I wanted to play. He looked forward to running with me around our rural neighborhood. I would put him on a leash, and he would pull me around the two-mile course. Happy was truly a boy's best friend.

One day while enjoying our usual run, a German shepherd came blazing out of nowhere. He had broken loose from the rope that tied him to a tree (bad human more than bad pet!). He attacked Happy, pulled the leash from my hand, and ripped him to pieces before my very eyes. I was in shock, but quickly the adrenaline and stupidity kicked in. I wildly ran into the midst of the massacre, screaming and trying to beat the dog off Happy. Amazingly, I scared the German shepherd away without getting bitten myself, but Happy was not so lucky. He lay motionless in a pool of blood on the pavement. Fearfully, I reached out to touch him and when I did, he let out a little whimper. The worst moment was when I picked him up and saw how badly he was hurt. I was sick to my stomach and scared to death, but I knew I had to get him to a vet as quickly as possible. I was almost to the halfway point about a mile from home. No one was around to help. The only option was to pick him up and start running. He weighed about thirty pounds, and I was a small, skinny thirteen-year-old kid. My arms began to ache, but I pressed forward. I was being strengthened by my deep love for Happy and by the urgency of his situation.

I arrived home gasping for breath but focused on getting him to the vet. My parents were out of town at a Christian convention on the other side of the country in San Francisco. Aunt Dru quickly came to my aid as she pulled out her white, 8-cylinder, 1968 Chevy Impala. With Happy in my lap wrapped in a towel we blasted off. We arrived at the vet's office in a few minutes, and they quickly took him into surgery. We waited for what seemed like an eternity until the vet came out to say they had been able to save Happy. However, it would be touch and go for the next several days, and Happy would need to stay in their care for up to a week.

Heading home for the night we were tired, but relieved. Aunt Dru called my parents to tell them about the day's events, unaware I was listening on the other phone. She told them it looked like Happy would make it, but the entire bill would be at least $700.00 (an enormous amount for my family in 1980). My father snapped, "Dru, why didn't you just let that dog die?"

I jumped into the conversation, "Dad, if that's what that Christian convention is teaching, you better just come home."

My father took that rebuke—maybe the only one I ever gave him—and never said a negative word about the cost. Happy did make it. He came home, but he never regained his full strength. He continued to live with my Aunt Dru after we returned to Belize and died a few years later. Why did Happy being injured hurt me so badly? As we said earlier, "To love is to be vulnerable."

Pets touch our hearts in a unique way. They can elicit love from some of the grumpiest of people. People that do not even like other people can surprise you how much they love their Chihuahua or their Siamese cat. I do not comprehend the depths of the love-evoking power pets have, but I know it's real. As a young adult, I heard something that helped me understand it better. It came from that profound source of wisdom, *Beverly Hills, 90210*. As I remember it, one of the characters had both a pet and a parent to die fairly close to each other. This young woman was deeply stirred when her pet died, but she was stoic at the death of her parent with whom she had a troubled relationship. Because this obvious disparity worried her, she sought advice from a friend. The friend said, "With people our relationships are complicated and often conflicted, but with our pets it's all about love — pure and simple." I am not saying this is how it should be, but there is a kernel of truth in what she said. **Therefore, if you experience a pet's true love, it is worth finding the source of that love.**

Skeptics say you can't love an animal, but the Bible indicates that people, can and do, love all kinds of things. In fact, loving anything more than God is wrong. That is called "idolatry." God alone deserves our ultimate allegiance. The biblical concept of love is not merely a warm feeling for someone, but a whole-hearted commitment to the well being of that person. It is "a love" demonstrated by action, making the one you love a priority in your time, thoughts, feelings, and actions.

God desires and demands such a love from us. We are told to, *"Love the Lord your God with all your heart and with all your soul and with all your strength and with all your mind, and your neighbor as yourself" (Luke 10:27).* At first glance, this command from Jesus looks like *good* news, but it is actually *overwhelming* news. Why? We break this mandate from Jesus in countless ways every day, often simply by forgetting God. Hours pass with no thought of Him, and longer still, not seeking to honor, thank, or serve Him. This law of love is ultimately bad news. This is one standard we cannot keep in our own power. If our relationship with God is made right through the law of loving God and others perfectly, then we are all doomed.

At that moment of despair, we hear the good news, the Gospel, *"In this is love, not that we have loved God **but that he loved us** and sent his Son to be the propitiation for our sins" (1 John 4:10).* The heart of the Gospel is the heart of God, which is a heart of love. We generally love people who *love* us and rarely love people who *hate* us. The gospel shows us a different kind of love, one that is extended by God toward rebels who are His enemies. As the Bible says, *"While we were enemies we were reconciled to God by the death of his Son" (Romans 5:10a).*

When we ask ourselves why God sent His Son to die for us, the final answer is *His great love.* We are tempted to think it is because we are so special, so cuddly, and so cute like our animals, but that is *not* the Bible's answer. We are sinners, rebels, and enemies of God. The Gospel reveals that God's motivation is love, self-giving and self-sacrificing love. That love, when directed toward undeserving sinners, is called *grace.* That love, when it withholds and redirects our punishment onto His Son, is called *mercy.* Why do we receive grace and mercy? Not because we are worthy, but because God is great!

God's love is not defined by our concepts and practices of love. His love is the standard that should define our love. His love is not sentimentality, nor does His love discard His justice. The Bible teaches that God holds and maintains all of His manifold attributes in perfect balance and harmony. His love is foundational but does not diminish or conflict with His righteousness. **His love is *holy*, as are all His attributes.** The holy character of His love means it is a love set apart, unique, and absolutely pure. The love of God sent Christ to die on the cross. At that cross, God's righteous anger against our sin was satisfied (propitiated). **Jesus took upon himself, not only our sin, but also our punishment.** As the center of the Gospel, the death of Jesus stuns us when we meditate on its depth. His cross is the place where righteousness and peace kiss. It is the place where God's love is extended to us and the place where God's justice is satisfied. The Gospel never ceases to humble and to amaze.

We have been mercifully rescued, adopted, trained, and cared for by the love of God in Christ. We are now called to live a life of ever-increasing love for Him and for others. In his first letter John says we are fooling ourselves if we claim to love God, but we do not love our brother. The love of God is designed, not only to flow *into* us, but also to flow *out* of us. The evidence that God's Spirit lives inside of us is a growing love that manifests itself in joy, peace, patience, kindness, goodness, faithfulness, gentleness, and self-control. That love makes us willing to sacrifice ourselves for others, even our enemies. **We love because He first loved us.** I am confident you already love your animals. Wouldn't it be a disgrace to love the creature and not the Creator? God is love, and if you want to know love truly and fully, you must know Him.

Earlier I quoted C.S. Lewis, "to love is to be vulnerable." In essence that does not apply to God. He is invulnerable to failure, loss, or being thwarted in any way. Everything He purposes, He does. Everything He wants, He gets. Nevertheless, John says of Jesus, *"He was in the world, and the world was made through him, yet the world did not know him. He came to his own, and **his own people did not receive him"** (John 1:10-11).*

Why would we reject this gift of love? Why would we reject this gift of life? Why would we reject Jesus?

John explains, *"And this is the judgment: the light has come into the world, **and people loved the darkness rather than the light** because their works were evil" (John 3:19).* No matter what we think of ourselves, apart from God we have a love problem. If we hear the good news of God's love for us in Jesus Christ and reject it, what does that say about us? Our true love has been revealed, and it is the darkness. Everyday of their lives, humans can and do love darkness because it allows them to continue blindly in their pursuit of a self-directed life. The love of God is not only something to talk about, but it is a gift to be received. Therefore, to reject Jesus is to reject God's gift of love.

The Gospel is not merely a message to be heard; it is a message to be believed. The Apostle John clearly states, *"That you may believe that Jesus is the Christ, the Son of God, and that by believing you may have life in his name (John 20:31).* Do you believe? Have you received? God's love has come down to us. **You cannot earn or merit a right relationship with God by your good works. Being reconciled to Him is an undeserved gift to be received by faith, from the first moment to the last.** By faith, take hold of the hand that was pierced for you. If you come to Him, He will never cast you away.

Don't fail to identify the source of all love. Don't fail to find a love that never fails. Don't fail to be loved and to love the One who made you and who made all creatures great and small. Follow the stream back to its source and trace the painting back to the original. Connect the momentary back to the eternal. When you do, what will you find? **Jesus Christ! He *is* the greatest demonstration of God's love!**

The author with Indy and Fionn

David and Jennifer with Kelsey, Fionn, and Indy

Indy, ready for school

Dancing with Fionn

Fionn Connal

Chapter Eight

COMPANIONSHIP
Experiencing the Joy of Togetherness

And if I go and prepare a place for you, I will come again and will take you
to myself, that where I am you may be also.
(John 14:3)

What is man without the beasts?
If all the beasts were gone, men would die from a great loneliness of spirit.
Chief Seattle

"Psst! Your bag is moving," whispered my classmate from across the aisle. We were sitting in a lecture about the theology of Augustine of Hippo when he noticed my bag was shaking.

I whispered, "Don't worry; it's my dog, Indy." His eyes opened wide as saucers. I'm not sure he approved of a dog studying theology, but what better theologian for Indy to study than the theologian of hippos? Little did I know that Indy, who had been my present to Jennifer on our first wedding anniversary, would end up teaching me so much about companionship.

During four years of seminary in Texas, our Yorkshire terrier Indy was our constant companion. He often went to school with me and always sat with me while I studied at home. Even though he was tiny, he was in great physical shape and loved to go on long walks every day. He especially enjoyed riding with us in the car, always ready to climb into his special perch on my neck. Part of our time in Texas we lived in a sketchy neighborhood, but Indy was an outstanding guard dog. He would bark like crazy at anyone who came to the door, "working himself into a frenzy" when they rang the doorbell.

On one occasion, we even took Indy with us to a dollar movie. We got him into the theater, undetected in his small bag, and everything was going great. We were well into the movie, and Indy had been "as good as gold and as quiet as a church mouse" when Jennifer and I both saw it coming. On the screen, a man was approaching the door of a neighbor's house. We cringed as the man's hand reached toward the doorbell, and sure enough, as he pressed that doorbell, Indy started barking wildly. We tried to shush him and then to cover his barking by feigning a fit of coughing. Soon he quieted down, and happily no one reported us. Needless to say, that was the last time we ever took him to the movies.

Indy was a great companion until his final breath. From Indy I learned much about the power of *simply being present* and the *joy of togetherness*. He enjoyed being with us, and we enjoyed being with him. Many of you can attest to the profound joy you have experienced from years of companionship with your pets. Life together is a rich blessing, in both the good times and in the hard times. With our pets, we enjoy sitting together, walking together, and playing together. Oh, how wonderful is the deep contentment of simply being together with those whom we love!

The Bible is a story about companionship. It begins with the One God who is eternally in three persons. The Triune God in His essence is *relational*—the Father relating to the Son and to the Holy Spirit. All relationship flows from them. Because we are made in God's image, we are also relational beings. In the Bible the first thing God declared to be "nc   d" is man being alone. The animals could not satisfy Adam's de   relationship, so God created Eve. The marriage relations.   an and woman provided greater intimacy. However, th   d relationship was between mankind and God. God   m and Eve in the Garden in the cool of each day, but   od on the day they sinned. The Bible tells us that Go   n, *"Where are you?"* Adam timidly replied, *"I hea   ou in the garden, and I was afraid, because I was*   *myself"* (Genesis 3:9-10). **That's what sin does.   elationship with God. It makes us hide from Him.**

Nevertheless, the perfectly pure God set a plan in motion to find impure, hiding humans and to bring them back into relationship with Him. The culmination of that story is God the Son taking on flesh to reconcile us to God the Father. We have called that "the rescue." God adopted us into His family and is now training us to be like His Son. He does all of this from a heart of great love—a heart that desires and offers deep and daily companionship with Himself.

Jesus' final promise to His disciples is that *He will be with them* to the very end of the age, yet He leaves. So how does He keep His promise of constant companionship? Jesus explains, *"And I will ask the Father, and he will give you another Helper, to be with you forever, even the Spirit of truth, whom the world cannot receive, because it neither sees him nor knows him. You know him, for he dwells with you and will be in you. I will not leave you as orphans; I will come to you" (John 14:16-18).*

If you have trusted Christ as your Savior, he graciously fills you with His Holy Spirit day by day. **Christ is present today in the lives of believers *through* His Holy Spirit.** He dwells with us and in us. The Divine Helper, speaking by and with God's Holy Word, guides us into greater understanding of Jesus Christ. The Holy Spirit *shows* us our sin, *bears* sweet-tasting fruit through us, *gives* us gifts for service, *empowers* us to be bold witnesses for Christ, and *strengthens* us for anything we might face. In other words, the Holy Spirit is the Divine Person through whom we have daily companionship with God. Because the Holy Spirit and the Father and the Son are one, we have fellowship with all three. This Divine Helper, the Holy Spirit, is essential for the Christian life. He applies *to* us all that Jesus accomplished *for* us. It is the Spirit in us who gives us the confidence that God is our Father. It is the Spirit in us who makes us miserable when we sin and stray from God. It is the Spirit in us who makes us delight in the joy of fellowship with God. This is a moment-by-moment companionship, of which the Bible declares, *"If we live by the Spirit, let us also walk by the Spirit" (Galatians 5:25).*

When we struggle against sin, it is the Spirit in us warring against that sin. As the Apostle Paul says, *"For the desires of the flesh are against the Spirit, and the desires of the Spirit are against the flesh, for these are opposed to each other, to keep you from doing the things you want to do" (Galatians 5:17).* The Holy Spirit, our powerful ally in the battle against sin, is our only hope for true spiritual growth.

We need to be filled with the Spirit every single day. The Bible exhorts, *"Don't be drunk with wine, because that will ruin your life. Instead, **be filled** with the Holy Spirit" (Ephesians 5:18, NLT). "**Be***

94

filled" is a second person plural imperative present passive verb. Wow! That's a headache-inducing mouthful. If you will hang with me, you will see why it matters. The "second person plural" means this command is for all Christians, not an elite few. The "imperative" means it is not an option, but a command. The "present" means it is for each and every day of our lives. The "passive" means the filling is done *to* us, not *by* us. Our posture is one of receiving.

Our part in this divine/human companionship is both avoiding some things and embracing others. We seek to avoid the distractions that can so easily fill us, leaving no room for the Spirit of God. **Instead, we embrace the Spirit by asking Him to fill us and by yielding to His filling—*each and every day.*** When we do not turn away from sin, we grieve and quench the Spirit in our lives, no longer experiencing His presence. James puts it simply, *"Draw near to God, and he will draw near to you" (James 4:8).*

Our present companionship with God is wonderful, but the companionship that lies ahead is greater by far. Jesus tells his disciples, *"And if I go and prepare a place for you, I will come again and will take you to myself, that where I am you may be also" (John14: 3).* One day we will be *with* Jesus. We will see our Savior face to face, and we will be with Him forever. Our companionship with God will only intensify in the future. Jesus expressed this, *"Father, I desire that they also, whom you have given me, may be **with me** where I am, to see my glory that you have given me because you loved me before the foundation of the world" (John 17:24).* Jesus desires for us to be with Him. He desires, *and promises,* full companionship forever!

Paul comforts grieving believers with the reality of future companionship by saying, *"For the Lord himself will descend from heaven with a cry of command, with the voice of an archangel, and* *with the sound of the trumpet of God. And the dead in Christ will rise first. Then we who are alive, who are left, will be caught up together with them in the clouds to meet the Lord in the air, and so we will always be **with the Lord.** Therefore encourage one another with these words"* (1 Thessalonians 4:16-18). Our future is one of being with the Lord. Our deep need for companionship will be *fully* met when *finally* we are with Jesus Christ. We will never again be lonely. We will never again be apart.

Amazingly, the Bible doesn't even stop there. Remember the rupture that occurred between God and us in Eden? We were forced from the Garden, and heaven and earth were separated. God made this world, and ultimately, it *is* under His control, but an evil occupying force—Satan and his demons—has been wreaking havoc for millennia. Thankfully, that occupation will end the day Satan and all who side with him are thrown into the lake of fire. On that day we will hear, *"A loud voice from the throne saying, 'Behold, the dwelling place of God is with man. He will dwell with them, and they will be his people, and **God himself will be with them** as their God'"* (Revelation 21:3). Paradise will be fully regained! We will experience **the joy of never-ending togetherness** with Him. This "togetherness" is so profound that it is referred to as marriage. Our deepest longings for companionship will finally be fulfilled in the God who created both the animals and us. Praise His Name Forever!

Chapter Nine

PRECIOUS MEMORIES
Delighting in the Wonderful Moments of Life

I remember the days of old; I meditate on all that you have done;
I ponder the work of your hands.
(Psalm 143:5)

When pet-people start talking about animals, it's all over. We regale you with tales of dogs, cats, horses, birds, ferrets, pot-bellied pigs, and the odd iguana or two. We tell you of encounters with animals in the wild: deer, squirrels, snakes, raccoons, bears, coyotes, foxes, hawks, and eagles. We remember fondly being mesmerized by ants working, by spiders weaving, by birds nesting, and by butterflies flitting. These experiences have deeply impacted us, and the mere mention of anything closely related to them brings back a flood of memories.

What are some of your favorite pet memories? Two of mine are rescue stories. On a spring day in 2011, Jennifer and I were riding back to the farm from the town where I pastor. It was raining "cats and dogs." We were on an isolated stretch of curvy road when

Jennifer yelled, "Watch out!" I swerved to miss some tiny animal blob crouching on the white line at the edge of the road. As we passed it, Jennifer exclaimed, "It's a kitten." We quickly turned around and hurried back, hoping that it had not been hit.

When we got to the little kitten, he was still alive. We stopped our car in the middle of the road and turned on the flashers. As we did, the kitten darted into the road and under our car. Speeding vehicles approached from both directions as I signaled for them to stop. Jennifer, kneeling on the wet pavement, tried to coax the kitten from under the car. He was not about to budge, except to snap and claw at her hand. Jennifer grabbed a pair of gloves, scooted on her belly underneath the car, and snagged the little guy. We hopped back in, soaked but glad that the kitten was out of danger. The line of oncoming cars hardly waited until our door was shut to speed away. The tiny kitten fit in the palm of Jennifer's hand, but he was so wet and wild that her hand was the one place he wasn't going to stay. He weighed all of six ounces and was chilled to the bone. We found a warm bag to put him in while Jennifer looked at me and questioned, "Back to town?"

I countered, "Why?"

"To take him to the rescue group," Jennifer answered.

Without hesitating I declared, "No way, that's *my* cat." She has never let me forget it.

In honor of the Royal Wedding that was approaching in England, we named him Prince William. In a matter of months he had grown into a big, healthy, and strong cat. We love him dearly, and he is a vital part of our family. He gets along great with the dogs and even treats Fiona like a mother. Every time he needs something, Jennifer jokes, "Why don't you take care of it; after all, he's *your* cat."

The second memory involves a turtle rescue. Jennifer has been an inveterate and intrepid turtle rescuer for years, but one of her craziest incidents happened in 2009. She was driving by herself and rescued a small turtle from the middle of the highway. She found no safe place nearby to release him, so she decided to bring him home. Putting him in the front passenger-side floorboard, she turned her attention back to driving. After a few minutes she glanced over to check on him, only to find he was gone. She worried about it all the way home, but she assumed the turtle was there, just out of sight. She was right. When she arrived home, we started looking for the turtle only to realize that he had climbed up the floorboard and gotten into the dashboard. We could feel him but were not able to extract him. We worked at it for a long time until we finally sought help from our neighbor Roger, who is skilled with all things mechanical. Eventually, we were able remove the turtle safely, but only after the entire dashboard had been ripped out. It wasn't funny then, but it is now as I think back on holding up that little turtle victoriously in a yard strewn with the pieces of our car's interior. I warned you; it is dangerous to get an animal-lover recounting memories.

Memory is a truly great gift from God. Augustine said, "Great is the power of memory, exceeding great O God, an inner chamber, vast and unbounded! Who has penetrated to its very bottom?" (Confessions, Bk. 10 Ch. 17). Even though we cannot plumb its depths, we often delight in immersing ourselves in its treasures. The psalmist says, "*I remember the days of old; I meditate on all that you have done; I ponder the work of your hands*" (*Psalm 143:5*). "Remembering" enables us to bring the past into the present. It allows us to reflect on the meaning of what has taken place. It helps us to live better in the future because we have pondered the lessons of the past. Socrates said, "The unexamined life is not worth living." Have you carefully examined your own life and considered what it means?

Modern life seems to conspire at every turn against deep and significant thought. We have a world of information at our fingertips, yet we rarely ponder life's true meaning. We seldom take time to think about the things that matter most. One of the reasons I am writing this book is to meditate on the meaning of more than two decades of life with pets. They are wonderful, but why? They genuinely touch my heart, but why?

God gave us memory to help us live more faithful and fruitful lives. It surprises me how often the Bible urges us to remember God and what He has done for us. For example, Deuteronomy 8:18-19 says, " *You shall remember the LORD your God, for it is he who gives you power to get wealth, that he may confirm his covenant that he swore to your fathers, as it is this day. And if you forget the LORD your God and go after other gods and serve them and worship them, I solemnly warn you today that you shall surely perish."* Memory enables us to realize everything comes from God, even our animals. If we are not *thoughtful* of our blessings, we will not be *thankful* for our blessings.

Thinking back over our lives with the eye of faith helps us to see the hand of God in every valley and on every mountaintop. We see His continual provision for us and for our animals. The Bible says, *"Are not five sparrows sold for two pennies? And not one of them is forgotten before God. Why, even the hairs of your head are all numbered. Fear not; you are of more value than many sparrows" (Luke 12:6-7).* The old hymn, His Eye Is on the Sparrow, which is based on these verses, encourages us with the reality of God's bountiful care when it states:

Let not your heart be troubled
His tender words I hear
And resting on His goodness
I lose my doubt and fear
Tho' by the path He leadeth
But one step I may see
His eye is on the sparrow
And I know He watches me
His eye is on the sparrow
And I know He watches me

The hymn writer speaks of a confidence that comes from remembering the goodness and faithfulness of God—seen both in our lives and in His Word. **Biblical remembering is not about dwelling in the past but about preparing for the future.**

One of my favorite Hebrew words is *"tiqwah."* It is translated as "hope" in verses such as Psalm 62:5, which says, *"For God alone, O my soul, wait in silence, for my **hope** (tiqwah) is from him."* The word *"tiqwah"* derives from the word for "cord" or "rope". Hope is portrayed as a rope held taut on each end. One end is pulled back into the past, and the other end is pulled firmly into the future—leaving a dynamic tension in the present. Memory pulls us back to see the hand of God in the past. We see His track record of perfect consistency. He does not change or need to change.

This kind of God-ordained remembering propels our minds into the future. We are confident of a good future because of His faithfulness in the past. God's character and promises are perfect and unchanging. This is the foundation of biblical hope. Hope is a fruit of careful and regular meditating on what God has done and what God will do. We learn that every moment of our life matters, and every moment of the world's history matters. Certainly, we are called to use our memories to trace the hand of God in our personal lives; however, that is not the most important use of our memory. Interpreting our lives by reflecting on our past is still a proposition fraught with failure. We ought to heed the old song that says, "Judge not the Lord by feeble sense...God is His own interpreter." If our personal lives are not the pinnacle of what we are to remember, then what is? The answer is the Gospel of God's saving grace for sinners like you and me. What better way to use our memories than to recount the saving acts of God?

What better to remember than the Gospel? Time started when God created the heavens and the earth. Each moment since has been pregnant with possibilities. After our leap into sin, God has been working in time to bring about our deliverance. The Father's plan came to fulfillment when the Eternal Son stepped out of eternity and into time, leaving His infinite position of power and splendor in heaven for the confines of a virgin's womb. He left the glory of His throne for the ignominy of a manger. A manger where animals fed became the first bed for the One through whom all creatures were made. This child was given the name Jesus, meaning "the salvation of the LORD." This child did not grow up in the centers of power, but in an out-of-the-way place of no importance called Nazareth.

His earthly father was not a rich man, but a hard-working carpenter, who taught the One who made the trees how to fashion them into objects for man's use. He learned with no great school to teach Him, learning all that truly matters from the word of His heavenly Father. Jesus can truly sympathize with our weaknesses. In every respect he was tempted as we are tempted, yet without sin. He never gave in to an evil thought or action. His holy life was marked by unparalleled perfection. His earthly ministry spanned three short years, and if *all* were told, the world could not contain it. He taught and healed and fed the multitudes throughout the hills of Galilee.

He entered the kingly city of Jerusalem riding upon a common man's donkey, not a warrior's stallion. He came not to reign and rule as King, but to suffer and die as Savior. He was "tried" unjustly and condemned by the chief Priest and by Pontius Pilate. He was led out the city gates to die on a Roman cross. He was numbered among the evildoers yet never having sinned. **He died with exceeding grace and extreme agony.** All the while He prayed to His Father in heaven prayers that have never been forgotten. So powerful was this dying man's undying love, even a thief upon a cross next to Him and a soldier below trusted Him. In those dark hours, they saw Him for who He truly is—the Light of the World!

The Gospel is of such central importance to the Christian life that Jesus gives us a visible, tangible way of regularly remembering it: the Lord's Supper. Jesus instituted that Supper on the night before his death as a permanent reminder of what He was getting ready to do and why He was going to do it. He used simple everyday elements, bread and wine, which have become unforgettable symbols of His love and grace for every generation of believers.

While reclining at the Passover table, Jesus took bread and wine and used them as object lessons, explaining the "what and the why" of the Gospel. The loaf and the cup become doorways into deeper fellowship with Him as we receive them by faith. The bread is a portrait of His body that was to be broken for us so that we might be made whole by Him and brought into the presence of God. The wine is a portrait of his blood that was to be shed in order to wash away our sins. This meal is the Gospel "seen and tasted." We, who are so easily distracted and discouraged, have been given powerful pictures of the good news of what Jesus did on our behalf. The Lord's Supper is such a simple act, yet it helps us to remember one of the most profound realities—the good news of how God has saved us through Jesus Christ. The Apostle Paul tells us what we are to remember in the Lord's Supper:

For I received from the Lord what I also delivered to you, that the Lord Jesus on the night when he was betrayed took bread, and when he had given thanks, he broke it, and said, "This is my body which is for you. **Do this in remembrance of me.***" In the same way also he took the cup, after supper, saying, "This cup is the new covenant in my blood. Do this, as often as you drink it,* **in remembrance of me.***" For as often as you eat this bread and drink the cup, you proclaim the Lord's death until he comes. (1 Corinthians 11: 3-26)*

Every memory from our personal history is transformed by this watershed event. The death and resurrection of Christ has dealt a lethal blow to death itself. By Christ's death we now live. Everything has changed. Even the worst memories of your life are healed as you realize that your sins are forgiven and your future is secured. The good, the bad, and the ugly are all swallowed up in this past event. Even now the death and resurrection of Jesus is pulling us forward toward an incredible future. **Biblical hope is a confident expectation of a divinely provided future.** Therefore, in the light of the gospel of Jesus Christ, we can ponder the pain and the pleasures of our past knowing they are not the final word. **We can say with confident hope, the best is yet to be!**

Bradys' log home on Shadowlands Farm

Prince William

Pet-lover in training

Margaret

Chapter Ten

AGING
Wisdom Learned from Growing Old

Just ask the animals, and they will teach you. Ask the birds of the sky, and
they will tell you...Wisdom is with the aged, and
understanding in length of days.
(Job 12:7,12 NLT)

Old age means realizing you will never own all the dogs you wanted to.
Joe Gores

Many kinds of animals live their lives in fast-forward mode. We've all done the math on our dogs that requires us to remember our 7 times table. We look at our 5-year old canine and ask, "Now what's 5 times 7?" Using our lives as the standard, we see them aging seven times as fast as we do. One dog year equals seven human years, or something like that. The pet that was born on what seems like yesterday is now old. They don't play like they used to play. They hobble where they used to run freely. Their hair begins to gray. They bump into things because their eyes are growing dim.

They experience changes in weight, either up or down. They begin to lose control of their bladder and bowels. The list of indignities could go on and on...

One of the dear momma cats, which we took into our family in 1995, was named Margaret. She was the sweet matriarch of our back porch. She lived there with an assortment of other cats, including one of her daughters. The others would often get into "cat fights" with each other and with neighboring felines—not Margaret. She carried herself with a royal dignity that put her above all such petty squabbles. Even if a bigger neighboring cat came to bother them, she would just stand there and calmly look at the attacker until he left. She wouldn't run. She wouldn't counter-attack. She would merely stand there and conquer her assailants with the power of "unflappability" (of all the superpowers, this is the one I desire). We do not know exactly how old she was when we adopted her, but she ended up living to be somewhere around 18 years old. She experienced serious kidney problems for the last years of her life. Sadly, her condition worsened to the point of needing subcutaneous fluid every day in order to stay hydrated, and it was so hard to watch her waste away. It's always hard to watch one of our beloved pets experience decline.

Often we pet owners are willing to spend our "last dollar" to help our animals. We love them and will do anything to ease their suffering. Rightly, we fight aging in both our animals and ourselves. At the end of the day, we expend vast amounts of time and resources in the struggle *against* aging, however we spend almost no time or resources in gleaning wisdom *from* aging. **If we are willing, we can learn more by contemplating aging than by fighting for youth.** Youth in a fallen world is a passing mist. The Bible informs us, *"Life is like the morning fog— it's here a little while, then it's gone"* (James

4:14, NLT). If we prayerfully ponder aging, we will find golden nuggets of wisdom. Moses expressed that sentiment when he prayed, *"Teach us to realize the brevity of life, so that we may grow in wisdom"* (Psalm 90:12, NLT).

A family member of mine recently made a striking statement, "I have taken classes to be prepared to do all kinds of things, but no one has helped me prepare to grow old." How true his statement rings to the experience of many of us! Aging is relegated to the realm of public ridicule and private pain. We quietly engage in a "quixotic quest" to avoid or reverse the ravages of time, doing all we can to hold back the inevitable flood of aging but to no avail. The aches, the pains, the wrinkles, the graying hair, and the half-empty prescription bottles on the shelf tell us we are fighting a losing battle. However, if we contemplate these signs, we can gain great wisdom. I often think about a line I heard many years ago in a Tennessee Williams play. The narrator says, of the young, rich characters at the center of the story, "they thought they had an infinite number of tomorrows."

Our pets are great teachers—able to free us from the illusion of unending youth—if only we will listen. They age before our very eyes, making it much harder to deny the reality of growing old. Their quiet acceptance of aging challenges us to rethink our relationship with the same process. In the Old Testament book of Job the writer prods us, *"Just ask the animals, and they will teach you. Ask the birds of the sky, and they will tell you. Speak to the earth, and it will instruct you. Let the fish in the sea speak to you... For the life of every living thing is in his hand, and the breath of every human being"* *(Job 12:7-10 NLT).* We can learn many vital life-lessons from our animals and from the Bible: our time is short, aging is inevitable, simple pleasures are best, and most importantly, our lives are in the hands of the One who made us.

The brevity of life, clearly shown through our animals, can help us to take stock of what really matters. We struggle with being worried about everything imaginable. We worry about money, health, jobs, relationships—anything and everything. We make strenuous efforts to get ahead in our careers, only to realize that the reward is a gold watch or some other silly trinket. Yes, our work *is* important, but often we succeed in it at the expense of other priorities. If I live as long as my father, my life is more than half over. It is high time for someone like me, and maybe like you, to nail down what is most important in life. What are you living for? There is not an infinite number of tomorrows for any of us. Perhaps you have been avoiding the truly significant questions about the meaning and purpose of life. Perhaps you have been so busy that you have failed in your obligation to find what matters most. **The Bible distills it down to loving God and loving others.** Are those "loves" the primary emphasis in your life? All of these reflections are evoked in us by realizing life's brevity.

Our animals also demonstrate that aging is inevitable. It is reasonable for us to make significant efforts to take care of our pets and ourselves. Would it not also be reasonable to make equal or greater efforts to learn about the nature of life and the nature of the Life-giver? These efforts at gaining wisdom can lead to a greater freedom and freshness at life's end than you had at the beginning. Though aging is inevitable, growth need not stop. I have met a number of people who seem to grow more youthful in spirit as they grow older in age. God's people, according to Psalm 92, *"Still bear fruit in old age; they are ever full of sap and green, to declare that the LORD is upright; he is my rock, and there is no unrighteousness in him" (Psalm 92:14-15).*

This is a beautiful portrait of the senior saint. My mom, who is one of these remarkable saints, *puns* it this way, "The older I get; the "sappier" I get." What keeps these older Christians alive and fruitful is their vital rootedness in God. Their vigor is not squandered on the transient things of this life but is invested in the eternal things of God. They joyfully tell anyone their secret of staying young—being rooted in God. My retired, but still young-spirited, mother boisterously declares, "I have a full-time job bragging on God."

The Apostle Paul encourages us to keep the big picture in mind when he says, *"So we do not lose heart. Though our outer self is wasting away, our inner self is being renewed day by day. For this light momentary affliction is preparing for us an eternal weight of glory beyond all comparison" (2 Corinthians 4:16-17).* We can grow *spiritually* stronger, even as we are growing *physically* weaker. Do you see how this "spiritual renewal" reorients our thinking about growing old?

Additionally, our animals teach us the importance of enjoying life's simple pleasures: a good meal, a long walk, a nice nap, or a close cuddle. We struggle, thinking we will be happy when we get the promotion at work, the new relationship, the exotic vacation, the nice car, or the beautiful house. In reality life's true joys are much simpler and more accessible. In fact, the Apostle Paul demonstrates that if we have the Lord, we can be content in any circumstance, even if we don't have life's simple pleasures. Paul says, *"For I have learned in whatever situation I am to be content. I know how to be brought low, and I know how to abound. In any and every circumstance, I have learned the secret of facing plenty and hunger, abundance and need. I can do all things through him who strengthens me" (Philippians 4:11-13).*

The final lesson is that every life is in God's hand. The life of every animal and every human. If you have peace with God through Jesus, being in God's hand is a great comfort. He will enable you to face any situation. He will comfort you in every condition. You will not be paralyzed by fear of the future but propelled by faith in the good God who provides your future. As a blood-bought child of God, one of the greatest encouragements about growing old is that it does not lead to a dead end of death, but it is an open door to life. Every ache and pain, every wrinkle and spot are not signs that our best is in the distant past but that our best is in the near future. We run the race of life, inspired and empowered by Jesus Christ. The Bible urges us to, *"Run with endurance the race that is set before us, looking to Jesus, the founder and perfecter of our faith, who for the joy that was set before him endured the cross, despising the shame, and is seated at the right hand of the throne of God (Hebrews 12:1-2).* **We are in a race, and that race is leading us home. Home is being with the one who loves us and sacrificed all for us, Jesus Christ.** We cannot give up. We cannot give in to discouragement. We must look up to Jesus, and He will bring us safely home.

We can face old age with confidence, not confidence in ourselves, but confidence in the God who will never forsake us. A line from a hymn has been a great blessing to me in recent years, helping me to remember that each day is another step nearer journey's end. It says, "I nightly pitch my moving tent a day's march closer home" (Forever With the Lord, James Montgomery). Closer Home! Closer Home! What sweet words! When I hear them they put a spring in my aging legs. I can make it another day. The Gospel assures me, I am headed home. What about you?

Chapter Eleven

DEATH
Grieved by Death's Long Reach

The last enemy to be destroyed is death.
(1 Corinthians 15:26)

Every animal-lover dreads the day their beloved pet takes its last breath. The sorrow over a pet's death can be so deep that one doubts ever recovering. Unlike the death of other humans, this grief is one that many around you do not understand; they just do not know how to comfort you. It is as if the non-pet people are saying, "Come on, just get over it; it was only a dog (cat or whatever)." We cannot "just get over it." What we feel is real and profound grief. However, we often feel embarrassed by our heartbreak, believing that we have no one with whom we can share our feelings.

Through my years as a pastor, people have timidly asked me, "My pet died; would you pray for me?" I am immediately filled with compassion because I understand their silent pain: few people to talk to, fewer still who truly understand, and no recognized way to mark their pet's passing. I am confident that a biblical understanding of death will comfort and strengthen you more than you can imagine.

On our farm we have a secluded, tree-lined terrace that is the final resting place for many of our animals. As we walk by their graves, our minds are filled with memories of times spent with that particular animal. We call their names: Indy, Fionn, Willie, Margaret, Colin, Megan, Gummy, Tee, Bart, Kahlua, and Penelope... We recall how they lived and how they died. Each one unique. Each one loved. Each one remembered.

Here is Fionn, our amazing Wolfhound, who quietly took his last breath in January of 2000, leaving a hole in our hearts that took years to fill. Over there is Bart, our muscle-bound bay horse, who wasted away before our eyes and dropped with a thud to the ground one sad day. Even writing these words brings the pain flooding back. Most of us pet owners can recall agonizing deliberations with vets about putting a suffering animal to sleep. We remember those weighty judgments; decisions, nevertheless, had to be made.

Sometimes, we even grieve in advance. Today, while throwing for Ari, our thirteen year-old Poodle who loves chasing the ball, I wonder when his last fetch might come. I can hardly stand it. In my mind I hear words from The Lion King asserting, "It's all just the circle of life."

Every fiber of my being revolts against that statement and says, "Death may be the way it *is*, but it is not the way it *should be*." Is this just wishful thinking on my part, or does the Bible actually address this topic?

Death *is* addressed throughout the Bible. In the first two chapters of Genesis, we read of a newly created world in which there is no death. However, when our first parents rebelled against God, death came crashing through the door, a righteous consequence of our sin. Earlier we considered a verse, which explains the presence of death, by saying, *"Therefore, just as sin came into the world through one man, and death through sin, and so death spread to all men because all sinned" (Romans 5:12)*. If we humans were not willing to trust and obey the Author of Life, we would taste death. The "earnings" from our rebellious life would be our own death and the death of every other breathing creature.

Chapter 5 of Genesis records names and length of life of a few of our earliest ancestors. For example, verse twenty-seven says, *"Thus all the days of Methuselah were 969 years, and he died" (Genesis 5:27)*. That's the longest recorded life span in the Bible, but Methuselah's age is not the most shocking part. The most shocking part of that verse is, *"And he died."* That terrifying refrain, *"And he died,"* is the constant chorus of woe that marks every life in that chapter and every life since. Well, almost every life. Enoch and later Elijah were "transported" to heaven without dying. They are the only known exceptions to the "rule of death." They serve to teach us that God is Master over His own rules. Even mighty death must submit to the will of the Almighty. Enoch and Elijah stand as quiet sentinels, pointing us to God's plan to destroy death.

Gladly, the Bible doesn't only tell us the bad news of sin and death, but more importantly, it tells us the good news of forgiveness and life in Jesus Christ. Paul exclaims, *"Our Savior Christ Jesus, who abolished death and brought life and immortality to light through the gospel" (2 Timothy 1:10b)*. **Jesus came to abolish death!** Death is no natural, beautiful part of the circle of life. It is an ugly, vile enemy that we brought into the world when we turned our back on God. Gratefully, God who is rich in mercy did not leave us in our trespasses and sin, but He came to us in Jesus Christ to make us alive forever. Yes, believers do still experience physical death until Christ returns, but when He does, our bodies will be resurrected and reunited to our already perfected souls.

In light of this, should we quietly accept death, or should we vehemently reject it? The Christian answer is: *both*. Ultimately, death is an enemy, but in Christ, it is a defeated enemy. Death's sting has been removed. In the words of the Apostle Paul, *"O death, where is your victory? O death, where is your sting? The sting of death is sin, and the power of sin is the law. But thanks be to God, who gives us the victory through our Lord Jesus Christ" (1 Corinthians 15:55-57).* Mighty death has been humbled. Our Savior is victorious. Death is no longer a dead-end street but a doorway into the joy-filled presence of God.

As Christians, we are taught that to be absent from the body is to be present with our Lord, yet we know God has work for us, here and now. That is why we can echo Paul's sentiments when he said, *"For to me to live is Christ, and to die is gain. If I am to live in the flesh, that means fruitful labor for me. Yet which I shall choose I cannot tell. I am hard pressed between the two. My desire is to depart and be with Christ, for that is far better" (Philippians 1:21-23).* Now we can face death with a strong faith in the person and promises of our Resurrected Rescuer, Jesus Christ! The Bible promises, *"The last enemy to be destroyed is death" (1 Corinthians 15:26).* We catch a glimpse of that soon-coming, resurrection morning when God, *"will wipe away every tear from their eyes, **and death shall be no more**, neither shall there be mourning, nor crying, nor pain anymore, for the former things have passed away" (Revelation 21:4).* Hallelujah! What a Gospel! Hallelujah! What a Savior! Amen.

So what about the death of our pets? How do we face that? What does the Bible say?

The Bible does not tell us directly what happens to animals after they die. We will examine what it says and implies about their after-life in the final chapter. Meanwhile, with a heartfelt desire to help you in your grief, I offer the following suggestions, believing they flow from biblical principles.

Each person should be given permission to experience and to express genuine and profound sorrow at the death of a beloved pet. Recently, I was reminded of the importance of this when the long arm of death reached into our home again. Remember the tiny kitten we rescued on the side of the road and named Prince William? He was the picture of health, and we fully expected him to live for twenty years with the vitality, nutrition, exercise, and love that marked his existence. He brought so much joy and laughter into our home and had firmly worked his way into our hearts. He was eighteen months old, and it was time for his rabies booster. We took him to the vet, who administers this shot routinely to hundreds of animals. Sadly, William had an adverse reaction to the vaccine. Despite our best efforts, our sweet William was dead ten days later. I had forgotten how deep and awful grief is. Many of our animals have been elderly and declining for years before their death, but with William there was nothing to lessen the dreadful blow. His was a death out-of-time. His was completely unexpected. His death seemed to come out of nowhere, and it hurt us so deeply. We wept and wept over him. Our hearts were as truly and thoroughly broken as if we had lost a human loved one. We continue to miss him more than words can express.

I know there are people who just can't understand this reaction to the death of a cat. As bad as it hurts, I would rather have a heart that loves too much than one that loves too little. I would rather have a heart that loves widely and deeply rather than narrowly and shallowly. When your heart is broken over the death of a pet, you do not need to apologize to anyone for your grief. Experience the pain and sorrow. Express that pain and sorrow because death truly is a vile and horrible enemy. Don't bottle up or short-circuit your thoughts and feelings. At the same time, don't expect everyone to sympathize with you. Many people just do not understand. Let them be responsible for their own reactions while you focus on being responsible for yourself. Don't put yourself on a timetable for when you must stop grieving because that time will come.

In fact, there is an entire book of the Bible, which is an extended expression of grief. Lamentations is an intense and poetic outpouring of heart-wrenching sorrow at the destruction of Jerusalem, the Temple, and the thousands who perished in the ruthless massacre by the Babylonians. Lamentations 1:16 says, *"For these things I weep; my eyes flow with tears; for a comforter is far from me, one to revive my spirit; my children are desolate, for the enemy has prevailed."* Reading the book of Lamentations makes us realize there are things that *should* make us grieve, and it is necessary for us to express our laments.

In the midst of this extremely dark period, we read one of the brightest statements of faith in the Bible, *"But this I call to mind, and therefore I have hope: The steadfast love of the LORD never ceases; his mercies never come to an end; they are new every morning; great is your faithfulness" (Lamentations 3:21-23).* Isn't it encouraging to know that others who have walked through deep, dark valleys of grief have found bright peaks of hope in the midst of their sorrow?

During our loss of Prince William, I re-learned that grief often links to other grief. For example, when you are deeply mourning the death of a pet, it may tap into former sadness that remains unresolved. Take that opportunity to deal with the former grief more thoroughly. Recognize that grief can be caused by any kind of loss, not just a death. The loss of a job, a relationship, a home, or even a dream can create grief that we often ignore. We may even think those things are not worthy of sadness. Unresolved losses will lurk around in the shadows of our heart until we acknowledge and express them. That is when we find that our grief over the death of a pet might actually unlock the door to a long-neglected cellar where unresolved heartbreak lives. Let it happen. It is a blessing in disguise. This is a unique gift to you from your now deceased pet.

Let's look beyond our emotions of grief to see the deeper biblical realities at work. I know that what I am getting ready to say is a hard pill to swallow, especially when you are in the middle of grieving. Read the following *only* if you are in the frame of mind to think deeply about why animals die. If today is not that day, put off reading this section until you are ready. You will know when it's time.

Why do animals die? Animals die because we humans brought death into the world through our sin and rebellion against God. This first became real to me as I dug a grave in the red clay soil of our farm to bury our cat Colin. He had once belonged to our neighbors. However, he enjoyed visiting our back porch and liberally spraying it with his unpleasant aroma. We asked our neighbors to fix him. They refused. Finally, we caught him and took him to the vet ourselves to be neutered. When we brought him back and released him, we thought we would never see him again. We were wrong; he was at our house early the next morning. When our neighbors moved a few months later, he stayed. He was a strong cat, full of life, and yet here I was burying him. I asked myself, why? It dawned on me that he died because I am a sinner. To put it more broadly, death came to animals because our forefather Adam sinned and brought death into our world. That is something we should mourn. Jesus says, *"Blessed are those who mourn, for they shall be comforted" (Matthew 5:4).* Biblical mourning is always intended to turn us from our sin toward the embracing of the free gift of forgiveness and life in Christ. In other words, legitimate grief is not a destination but a crossroads on the journey. The Bible spells out that reality, *"For godly grief produces a repentance that leads to salvation without regret, whereas worldly grief produces death" (2 Corinthians 7:10).*

Grief does not get the final word in the loss of our pets. As weighty as our grief is, it needs to be counterbalanced by a sense of profound gratitude. Your animal didn't create itself. It didn't come to you by chance. It didn't live its life independent of divine sustenance. Trace the gift back to the giver. It was God's gift from first to last. Keep in mind, *"Every good gift and every perfect gift is from above, coming down from the Father of lights with whom there is no variation or shadow due to change" (James 1:17).* Focus your thoughts on the wonderful times God gave you together, rather than just wishing for more. **Gratitude is a righteous antidote to grief.** Turn your mind to the reality of how blessed you are to have known your precious pet, and the tossing waves of sadness will finally reach the solid ground of gratitude. When you arrive at that point, you are ready to embark on whatever God has in store for you.

The entire grieving period beckons us to *careful reflection* on the meaning of life and death. Grief spurs us to ponder what is truly important. **The death of a pet can be one of the greatest**

opportunities for parents to discuss the reality of dying *and* the reality of new life in Christ with their children. As a pastor it has been enlightening to see how many children have their first exposure to death through the death of a pet. When a beloved pet dies, children feel genuine sorrow, which can serve to open their young hearts to listen to the Gospel for the first time. The Bible surprisingly advises us, *"It is better to go to the house of mourning than to go to the house of feasting, for this is the end of all mankind, and the living will lay it to heart"* *(Ecclesiastes 7:2)*.

Recently, a godly man in our church came to see me with tears in his eyes, saying that one of his dogs had been hit and killed by a car on the road in front of his house, and his children were heartbroken. He had taken that opportunity to teach them about death and new life in Christ. I knew that was only one of his many acts of faithful witness to them, but in a few months three of his four children publically declared their faith in Jesus and were baptized. We need to learn not to hide the reality of death from our children and not to ignore the reality of death for ourselves. Death becomes a teacher to all who will listen, pointing us away from the shifting sands of this passing world toward the solid rock of faith in Jesus Christ. Death becomes a wake-up call to stop living for the superficial and to start living for the truly important.

As a result of such reflection, recommit yourself to the joyful *embracing of each moment* of life as a gift. The rapidity with which most of our pets live and die is a constant reminder to live fully in each moment. This requires single-mindedness. It requires contentedness. It requires attentiveness. It requires a focus on others, not only on ourselves. It requires being more concerned about *giving* than *getting* as we, *"remember the words of the Lord Jesus, how he himself said, 'It is more blessed to give than to receive'" (Acts 20:35).* This world is always tempting us to focus exclusively on ourselves. We are constantly distracted. In the midst of such busyness, we need to learn the discipline of focus. I have wasted countless moments of life worrying about possibilities that never came to pass. I have squandered precious times with others because I was too preoccupied to give them my full attention. My animals are rarely that way. They live in the moment much more fully than do most of us. They live out the good advice, "wherever you are, be all there."

Our experience and the truth of Scripture teach us the futility of trusting in ourselves and in our ability to control life. Rather, we are called to a *total trust* in the goodness and greatness of God. Grief can wean us from our worldly distractions, preparing us for a greater confidence in God. We don't know all the future holds, but we know Him who holds the future. Gratefully, He is working everything together for the good of His children *(Romans 8:28)*. In our grief we need to hear the voice of Jesus calling from the tomb of Lazarus, *"I am the resurrection and the life. Whoever believes in me, though he die, yet shall he live, and everyone who lives and believes in me shall never die. Do you believe this?" (John 11:25-26).* Do you trust your future to Jesus? Remember, mistrust of God was the seed of our rebellion in the Garden of Eden. We must relinquish our attempts to control our fate and acknowledge that believers are in the best of hands: God's. In the words of Jesus, *"My sheep hear my voice, and I know them, and they follow me. I give them eternal life, and they will never perish, and no one will snatch them out of my hand" (John 10:27-28).*

In light of what we have learned, are there any biblically appropriate ways to mark the death of a pet? The Scripture does not suggest ceremonies to commemorate the death of an animal, but surprisingly, it does not contain much specific information regarding human funerals either. So I offer the following suggestions on the basis of general biblical principles, not specific biblical passages.

The first principle is that all creation belongs to God. There is no genuine distinction between the secular and the sacred. In the words of the Psalmist, *"The earth is the LORD's and the fullness thereof, the world and those who dwell therein" (Psalm 24:1)*. Therefore, to say that the death of people is important, but the death of animals is not, runs against the principle of both being made by God and belonging to Him. We need to regain a desire to see all of life through a biblical lens, even the death of an animal. Yes, it is clear they are not humans, but animals are beautiful works of God's hands, and we shortchange God's glory if we don't thank Him.

There is a valid distinction between what we do *officially* as Christ's church and what we do *informally* as Christians. We have no example or command of a service to mark the death of a pet in the Bible. The Church, which is called to worship God only according to His commands, should not create an official rite for the death of an animal. However, as individual Christians, we are called to worship God in all of our lives, so we would do well to mark the passing of a pet in God-honoring ways. I suggest you could have a time of prayer, Scripture reading, and sharing stories about your pet. It could include the pet's burial, or it could be a separate event altogether. Set aside time to thank God and to remember your pet. **All of life needs to be seen in its relationship to God.**

On the website, www.livinginthevertical.com, you will find a list of suggested scriptures and other ideas to commemorate the passing of your pet. When we pray, we are not praying for the deceased pet because it is already firmly in God's hands and needs no prayers. Instead, we are thanking God for creating and sharing that animal with us. Our prayers are prayers of gratitude. Additionally, we pray for wisdom and comfort. We pray that we will "lay to our hearts" the spiritual lessons God is teaching us in the midst of our sorrow. In those prayers we look to Jesus, the resurrection and the life, as our blessed hope. We share stories of our beloved pet: stories of birth, rescue, adoption, training, companionship, love, aging, and death. We speak of our hope in God and of our confidence in the good future He has in store for us and for all creation. As we do, God is honored, and we are comforted.

In conclusion, the death of our pets can be a very painful, but profitable experience. It profits us *if* we turn to God and find our hope in Him. In our grief, we are called to preach the good news of Jesus Christ to our own hearts. We agree with Scripture, *"Why are you cast down, O my soul, and why are you in turmoil within me? Hope in God; for I shall again praise him, my salvation and my God" (Psalm 42:1).* In that sad hour of your beloved pet's passing, when your heart is broken, look up, and you will find that God is there. He will never leave you. His presence will sustain you in that dark hour. His Gospel will give you hope. You are forever safe in the His strong arms!

Ari loves to fetch

Ari with Jennifer

Ari with David

Baby Burrito

Burrito

Burrito and Jennifer

Chapter 12

WHAT'S NEXT?
The New Heavens and Earth

And he who was seated on the throne said,
"Behold, I am making all things new."
(Revelation 21:5)

O ne of the most common pet questions I am asked is, "Do you think my pet will be in heaven?" Because people feel so deeply about this question, some are ready to reject God and Heaven if their animal will not be there. They feel like the person who rhymed, "No heaven will ever Heaven be; unless my cats are there to welcome me."

Perhaps they agree with Robert Louis Stevenson who said, "You think dogs will not be in heaven? I tell you, they will be there long before any of us." I understand these sentiments. However, as Christians, we base our beliefs on what the Bible teaches and not on our feelings, experiences, or best guesses.

The Bible teaches us the *souls* of believers go immediately into Christ's presence upon their death; we receive resurrected *bodies* upon Christ's return to earth. On that day, our bodies will become perfect and incorruptible like Christ's resurrected body. At this point, we need to *slow* down... We need to let the biblical portrait of heaven sink deeply into our minds and hearts, allowing that portrait to correct our misconceptions. I was never very thrilled about heaven. Frankly, it sounded boring: eternal choir practice, floating on clouds, streets of gold, pearly gates, and never-ending harp music. It seemed like one long, long church service from which we never get dismissed (note to self: shorten your sermons!). If a gray disembodied future sounds dull to you, maybe you can understand my sentiments.

When we examine what the Bible *actually* teaches, we realize the new heavens and earth will be anything but boring. It will be the most fully embodied experience imaginable. This is why ancient Christian creeds (statements of belief) state clearly that the Bible teaches the *bodily* resurrection of the dead. I have found many Christians who think the Bible merely teaches the immortality of the soul, like the ancient Greeks. However, the Bible sets forth so much more. Imagine a purified and perfected earth: pristine air, water, and soil. A place that is like earth today, only better, unimaginably better than our currently fallen planet. Gone will be all the pollution, decay, and death.

Paradise not only will be regained, but also will be enhanced beyond measure. Joyfully, in our resurrected bodies we will be perfectly devoted to carrying out the will of God our Father. The Apostle Paul delivers us from our ignorance explaining, *"For we know that the whole creation has been groaning together in the pains of childbirth until now. And not only the creation, but we ourselves, who have the firstfruits of the Spirit, groan inwardly as we wait eagerly for adoption as sons, the redemption of our bodies" (Romans 8:22-23).*

There is much we could say about the new heavens and earth, and we need to be perfectly clear that what is yet to come is not a diminished version of what we have now. Rather, it will be a magnification and purification of our current earth. Our future existence will be very "earthy" indeed but without the sin and brokenness that is *in* and all *around* us. It will be far better than we are able to imagine.

Everything that is good in this life is a gift from God. God is the One who gives us loving families, loyal friends, delicious food, beautiful landscapes, and our amazing animals. Remember the passage from the book of James we saw in the last chapter about grief? It declares, *"Every good gift and every perfect gift is from above, coming down from the Father of lights with whom there is no variation or shadow due to change. Of his own will he brought us forth by the word of truth, that we should be a kind of firstfruits of his creatures" (James 1:17-18).* **Since our animals are good gifts from God in this "fallen" life, why should we expect Him to give us less in the "perfected" life to come?** These verses clearly state that the good God who gives these good gifts does not vary or change at all. In his outstanding book on heaven, Randy Alcorn says of God, "He's the *giver* of all good gifts, not the *taker* of them" (Heaven, pg. 385).

Additionally, the passage in James speaks of the redemptive power of God's word of truth, which is another way to describe the Gospel. James says that the word of truth is what has caused us to be spiritually born again. We are called the "firstfruits of his creatures," not the only fruits of his creatures. Although the Gospel is fundamentally for us, it ultimately benefits all other creatures as well. That word of truth, the Gospel of Jesus Christ, redeems and reconciles humans to God, but it finally leads to the restoration of the whole creation. The definitive goal of Jesus' work is, *"to reconcile to himself all things, whether on earth or in heaven, making peace by the blood of his cross" (Colossians 1:20).* Certainly, that must include God's wonderful creatures, the animals.

In C.S. Lewis' biblically based novels about Narnia, I hear the truth about heaven in <u>The Last Battle</u> ringing through the lips of the Unicorn, "I have come home at last! This is my real country! I belong here. This is the land I have been looking for all my life, though I never knew it till now. The reason why we loved the old Narnia is that it sometimes looked a little like this." In other words, the new heavens and earth will not feel alien to us but even more real, more vivid, and more like home.

Now back to our questions about pets being in heaven. I think the fundamental question is easier to answer, "will animals be in heaven?" The answer is a resounding: YES! The most obvious example is Jesus' mode of transportation for his return to earth. We read, *"Then I saw* **heaven** *opened, and behold,* **a white horse!** *The one sitting on it is called Faithful and True" (Revelation 19:11a).* The verses go on to say that all the armies of heaven follow Jesus riding white horses. I take these verses literally. I know there are interpreters of Scripture who believe this is only symbolic language. I ask them, "What makes it impossible for the horses mentioned to be real animals?" Wouldn't it be misleading to speak of horses being in heaven if they were actually banished? I think the burden of proof lies with anyone who seeks to set forth a heaven *without* animals. Why would the unchanging God change horses now?

Isaiah describes a coming golden age, *"The wolf shall dwell with the lamb, and the leopard shall lie down with the young goat, and the calf and the lion and the fattened calf together; and a little child shall lead them. The cow and the bear shall graze; their young shall lie down together; and the lion shall eat straw like the ox... for the earth shall be full of the knowledge of the LORD as the waters cover the sea" (Isaiah 11:6-9).* Do you notice the animals will not hurt each other? They will eat side by side, happily co-existing without the predator/prey mentality of this present fallen age. Even the meat-eating lion will become a confirmed vegetarian. Why? Because there will be a massive increase in everyone's personal knowledge of God.

Frequently, "animal images" are used to describe Jesus in heaven. He is called "the Lion of Judah" and "the Lamb that was slain." It would not make much sense to use animal imagery if they were not there. All the evidence and logical inferences point us to the conclusion that animals will populate the new heavens and earth. They will continue to be an important part of God's rich and diverse universe.

The more difficult question is, "Will my specific pet be in heaven?" Let's be clear that the Bible does not directly address this question. In this case we can come to a better understanding but no definitive conclusions. One of the most frequently raised objections to specific animals being in heaven is the assertion that they do not have a "soul." I readily agree that animals do not have a human soul but hasten to add that the Scripture does refer to their inner life using the word translated as "soul." For example, the Old Testament refers to animals as having a *nephesh*, which can be translated as "soul," "spirit," or "breath of life" (Genesis 1:30, 2:7; 6:17; 7:15,22). That may merely reference the fact that they are alive, however *nephesh* certainly includes them in a special class with humans as those having the "breath of life." We know that whatever their souls are, they are different from a human soul, but they do have some kind of internal life. What I am saying is that you *cannot* disqualify animals from the world to come on the basis of their not having a "soul" when that is the very term used in the Bible to refer to their inner life. The question that still faces us is, does each animal's "inner life" continue after death, or do they simply cease to exist?

The Bible clearly teaches us that each and every animal is created, known, provided for, cared for, and remembered forever by God our Heavenly Father. Jesus teaches this. Listen to what he says in Matthew 10:29, *"Are not two sparrows sold for a penny? And not one of them will fall to the ground apart from your Father."* Literally, the word "apart" means "without." Therefore, not even the smallest of animals dies outside of the Father's loving presence. In Luke 12:6, Jesus makes a similar point, *"Are not five sparrows sold for two pennies?* ***And not one of them is forgotten before God.***" This is a profoundly moving truth. God never forgets any animal that He created. Not one, not ever! That includes your specific pet. They matter to Him, and if they are forever on His mind, why should we think that they would not also be in His restored world?

However, the most important thing is to trust God no matter what. There are numerous issues not addressed by the Bible, and as believers we are called to trust Him with the things He has not chosen to reveal to us. We know that God is good, and Jesus has said, *"Behold I am making all things new" (Revelation 21:5).* That may include our specific animals, but ultimately that is His decision and not ours. We need to trust Him. We know that He works all things together for the good of those who love Him and have been rescued by Him. Let's get rid of the mistrust and believe that whatever is next will be glorious and even better than the best we have ever experienced. In the precious words of Scripture, *"Trust in the LORD with all your heart, and do not lean on your own understanding. In all your ways acknowledge him, and he will make straight your paths" (Proverbs 3:5-6).*

God is all-powerful, and He is certainly *capable* of bringing back our specific animal friends if He so chooses. The Angel Gabriel reminds us, *"For nothing will be impossible with God" (Luke 1:37)*. The Psalmist teaches, *"Whatever the LORD pleases, He does, in heaven and on earth, in the seas and all deeps" (Psalm 135:6)*. Therefore, we should not limit God as to what He can do.

However, above every other reality, Heaven is about being with God. Remember the Gospel? Peter summarizes those glad tidings, *"For Christ also suffered once for sins, the righteous for the unrighteous, **that he might bring us to God**..."* (1Peter 3:18). Jesus died for our sins, not just that we could be forgiven, but that we would be brought all the way home into the presence of God. Jesus with His nail-scarred hands leads us up to the awesome throne of God. There we find our Eternal Father.

We struggle now to grasp that being in the presence of God is what we will most desire in the coming age, and that is exactly where we will be. In the words of the Puritan preacher, Thomas Goodwin, "Heaven would be Hell to me without Christ." The very heart of heaven is God, and in our future sinless state we will desire Him above every other desire.

In his book The Four Loves, C.S. Lewis makes this point beautifully:

> We are made for God. Only by being in some respect like Him, only by being a manifestation of His beauty, loving-kindness, wisdom, or goodness, has any earthly Beloved excited our love. It is not that we have loved them too much, but that we did not quite understand what we loved. It is not that we shall

be asked to turn from them, so dearly familiar, to a Stranger. When we see the face of God we shall know that we have always known it. He has been a party to, has made, sustained and moved moment by moment within, all our earthly experiences of innocent love. All that was true love in them was, even on earth, far more His than ours, and ours only because His. In heaven there will be no anguish and no duty of turning away from our earthly Beloveds. First, because we shall have turned already; from the portraits to the Original, from the rivulets to the Fountain, from the creatures He made lovable to Love Himself. But secondly, because we shall find them all in Him. By loving Him more than them we shall love them more than we now do.

Wow! Did you get that?

We love whatever we love here on earth because it flows from God. As we love Him more in the age to come, we will be able to love all others more purely and perfectly!

Finally, God's plans have always been filled with unexpected twists and turns. Who could have ever imagined that He was going to save the world by sending His Son to die in our place? God's redemptive plan has been filled with surprises from the beginning. Therefore, I look forward to the joys of a restored heaven and earth with great anticipation. I look forward to seeing our Savior, Jesus Christ, face to face. I look forward to meeting many of you pet-lovers, who are also God-lovers. At the end of the day, I look forward, with great trust in a good and often-surprising God, to those unexpected blessings that lie in our future. I hope that around the corner of some golden street, our beloved pets will come bounding toward us: healed, restored, and filled with joy as they leap into our arms. **I can hardly wait to see how God is going to weave everything together for our good and for His glory!** Even though the Bible does not tell us everything He has prepared for those who love Him, it does tell us enough that we can be confident what lies ahead is far better than we could ask or imagine.

What if we all end up happily surprised that our pets are in heaven? The question remains: **Will _you_ be there to meet them?** What a heartbreaking tragedy if you are not! A tragedy that is unnecessary and completely avoidable. The Bible assures us, *"everyone who calls on the name of the Lord will be saved" (Romans 10:13).* God has provided the perfect way home, if only you will take it. Jesus boldly declared, *"I am the way, and the truth, and the life. No one comes to the Father except through me" (John 14:6).* Do not miss Heaven! Do not miss the wonderful surprises that lie ahead. Do not miss out on Jesus making everything new.

As we've seen, we can't answer every question about the future, but we can be sure the best is yet to come. When it does, everything that has breath will be praising the Lord! I hope and pray your voice will be among the chorus of the redeemed. **Together, we will praise God for the good news of salvation, the Gospel of Jesus Christ, which is for all people,** *even pet-lovers.*

Headed home!

ACKNOWLEDGEMENTS

T his book would not exist without my wife Jennifer. Its pages flow directly from our life together. Its stories are our stories. I have learned more about God from Jennifer than anyone else. I have learned more about animals from Jennifer than anyone else. Together, we have laughed and cried on a daily basis over our wonderful animals. "Thank you, Jennifer! I love you and am deeply grateful for you. After the Lord, you have been my greatest blessing in life."

Several people generously helped me edit the manuscript. They caught grammatical errors and made numerous suggestions about style and content. "Thank you, James, Pam, and Brittany!" Others of you read individual chapters, prayed for me, and encouraged me along the way. You know who you are. "Thank You, All!"

but my bestest editor throughout has been my mother-in-law, Jane. For and yet, she has been my faithful "fanboy." She read my rough draft, which I thought was the final manuscript, and together we spent a *little* time polishing it. "Thank you, Mrs. J, an' ifn' it twern't fer ya hepn'me I'da neva thunka awh'lah dem puurrty waayza straanging werds."

I would also like to thank three photographers whose pictures of our animals appear in this book. **N. Johnson** came to our farm several years ago and took many beautiful photographs. "Thank you for helping us to preserve some very precious memories!"

One day in 1995, **Deni McIntyre** photographed us with the animals we had at that time. What resulted from Deni's creativity that day were several iconic images that truly express the depths of what our life with animals has been like. "Thank you, Deni!"

A long time friend, **Chris Smith**, of Chris and Cami photography, took the remarkable photograph of our log home in the winter. "Chris, your artistry is amazing. Thank you! You and Cami are not only wonderful people, but your love for animals makes you true kindred spirits."

Above all, I want to thank the Lord God, Maker of Heaven and Earth. I believe He gave me the idea for this book. I offer it up to Him as a sacrifice of praise. "Father, thank you for making the world, and thank you for redeeming the world through your Son, Jesus Christ. Thank you for saving me through your Gospel in the power of your Holy Spirit. May this book serve to increase your praise and honor among the pet-lovers of this world." AMEN!

CPSIA information can be obtained at www.ICGtesting.com
Printed in the USA
BVOW06s1107021115

425039BV00003B/5/P